WHY DON'T YOU
LISTEN TO
WHAT I'M NOT SAYING?

WHY DON'T YOU LISTEN TO WHAT I'M NOT SAYING?

Judith Milstein Katz, Ed.D.

ANCHOR PRESS/DOUBLEDAY
GARDEN CITY, NEW YORK
DOUBLEDAY CANADA LIMITED
TORONTO, ONTARIO
1981

The Anchor Press edition is the first publication of *Why Don't You Listen to What I'm Not Saying?*

Anchor Press edition: 1981

Library of Congress Cataloging in Publication Data

Katz, J. M. (Judith Milstein)
Why don't you listen to what I'm not saying?

Bibliography: p. 156
1. Social interaction. 2. Nonverbal
communication (Psychology) 3. Social perception.
I. Title.   Includes Index
HM291.K25   302
ISBN 0-385-17521-3   AACR2
Library of Congress Catalog Card Number 80–2965

For Sylvia, Paul,
and Jesse

Acknowledgments

My thinking about this book has been influenced by many friends and colleagues. Special thanks go to Andrew Effrat, Davida Egherman, Ron Egherman, Ruth Gilbert, John S. Katz, Keith Oatley, Judith Posner, and the late Peter Ziffo. Their readings of the manuscript, their encouragement, and their criticism have been invaluable. Most important my husband, John Stuart Katz, and my son Jesse deserve acknowledgment for having lived with my relentless analysis of our daily lives. They have offered a complexity and depth of experience which has enriched my life. I am grateful.

Contents

Part III

   The assumption that people do (or do not)
   change is self-fulfilling.

   The view that we make meaning has surprising
   consequences.

About This Book

Psychological theory affects our lives in ways we usually do not notice. Even when we do not read books about or study psychology, we are affected by the theories and assumptions of those who do. Over the last fifty years, we have been influenced greatly by two major psychological theories: Freudian theory, which emphasizes early experience, and behavior theory, which emphasizes the control of behavior through reward and punishment. These theories affect the way we relate to parents, raise and educate our children, and treat our friends and lovers. Though not aware that we do, we interpret people's actions in ways suggested by these popular and pervasive views. Our responses are influenced by our interpretations.

In academia, both these theories have been challenged. But research which changes the way we view the world is not yet part of public knowledge. There is at present a considerable gap between what the experts believe and what the public believes they believe. The difference between them is far from trivial.

Unfortunately, new research has had very little impact on our culture. To begin, there is no one unified theory to replace traditional frameworks. Data on which such a theory could be based come from diverse fields of study (child development, perception, and cognition) and have not been integrated. In any case, an alternative theory has not been elaborated or presented to the general public. This book offers such a framework which, for reasons that will be discussed later, I call Constructive Psychology. It integrates research from several areas, spanning many years, to present a theory which differs significantly from conventional assumptions. Changes in our assumptions affect the way we respond to events we encounter.

The primary impact of Constructive Psychology lies in its view that we interpret the world around us, that we "make" meaning rather than see it. Our perceptions are not, as traditional theories suggest, determined by events. Circumstances are ambiguous. Choice exists in how we interpret events and how we respond to what we see. The Constructive view differs from traditional views on these points: the acceptance of ambiguity and the recognition of choice. Combined, they change our view of man.

A simple incident illustrates both the importance of our assumptions and the pervasive influence of psychological theories in daily life. They influence virtually every interaction.

Several years ago while watching my son in the park I was surprised to see Lily, the mother next to me, jump up and interrupt her children, who had been wrangling over a plastic pail. She berated the younger boy, who was just over two years old, with a speech about jealousy: "Why do you want everything your brother plays with; just because he has a pail doesn't mean you will get one;

don't be jealous of your older brother because he's older; you're spoiled to want everything he wants."

I confess some surprise at her outburst. To begin, I did not see anything about her children's play that warranted interruption. I thought the tug of war was as much a part of their play as filling and emptying the pail had been minutes earlier. To my mind they were playing happily. To hers they were fighting competitively. Secondly, I was surprised that, seeing the fight as "real" rather than "play," she would attribute to it the complex meaning that she did. It's one thing to see a child fight over a pail, it's another to assume the fight reflects deep-seated and virtually unavoidable resentment and jealousy toward a brother. Thirdly, I was surprised she conveyed her assumptions to her children.

I was just as surprised by Lily's responses to my remarks. I said that by my standards she was lucky; what she called a fight was nothing compared to some fights I had seen. She looked at me as if I were insane and muttered that her kids fight like that all the time and it drives her crazy. She was clearly upset.

Then I asked how she knew the two-year-old was jealous. Jealousy is quite a complex emotion. Maybe he just wanted to play with the pail. Lily thought for a moment. She hadn't considered that possibility. Then she shook her head at me and said, "No, it's jealousy. It's sibling rivalry. I've been reading about it." It was sibling rivalry; the other parents on the bench agreed.

The incident at the sandbox is illustrative. The parents, both men and women with whom I chatted day after day, held clear ideas about psychology. They had devoured many books about child development and were quite well educated in popular psychology. As a result they had ready interpretations for behavior they observed in both children and adults, interpretations and theories which influenced how they responded to ambiguous situations. The difference between their views and mine were differences in theory. They responded as traditional psychologists. The books they read suggested specific assumptions for interpreting events—assumptions different from those under which I was operating. My assumptions, based on somewhat more recent research and a nontraditional framework, suggest different ways of dealing with children and adults.

Lily may not have interpreted her child's behavior correctly: the tug of war was ambiguous. But, having read a great deal about child development, Lily was prepared for and ready to see sibling rivalry. She, like other parents in our culture, read about sibling rivalry in a variety of popular books and magazines. They await its emergence, sometimes with dread but always with vigilance; traditional psychologists tell them to watch carefully for its appearance. This readiness increases the chance they will see what they expect. The same behavior displayed by unrelated children might look quite different: two kids squabbling about a pail. No deep psychological significance there. Having made her interpretation (based on prevailing theories) Lily saw no need to check that she was correct. (Various means of checking are discussed in later chapters.) Instead, she presented her interpretation as if it were fact. Her interpretation then becomes part of the information her children consider when they try to make meaning of each other's, and their own, actions. Lily's interpretation becomes a self-fulfilling prophecy. She would, I felt sure, end up with two competitive and jealous children. They would "drive her crazy" for years to come.

Lily's assumptions work in an interesting way. Her readiness to see rivalry affects what she learns from ambiguous behavior. Her assumptions affect her perception of events, how she feels about the events she encounters, and how she responds to people with whom she interacts. A different theory, stressing ambiguity and choice, would suggest alternative options, options which affect not only her relationship to her children but her friends, family, and colleagues—everyone with whom she interacts.

The first portion of this book presents the problem that each of us confronts. How, given ambiguity, do we interpret what we experience? The question is important. Social ambiguity is more pervasive and murkier than we generally think. The way we interpret affects our relationships.

New research and theory regarding learning shows why. The conventional view, that what we learn depends on events we encounter, is false. We are not, as Freudians and behaviorists assume, shaped by early events. Rather, what we learn is determined by assumptions we bring to situations. Our assumptions affect our experience and shape our interpretations in ways that are self-fulfilling. Because events are ambiguous, our interpretations usually fit; they seem to be correct, and influence later perception. Not early events, but the theories we ourselves construct to explain those events, affect us in later life.

"Ready, Get Set, See" (chapter 3) elaborates a related and especially intriguing view of perception—the theory of perceptual readiness. In addition to assumptions derived from early experiences, a variety of factors influence what we are ready see at different times and different places. Like an overeager racer who hears the gun before the starter signals, we are often perceptually overready. We see what we expect, not always what is there.

Awareness of ambiguity and readiness also changes our view of emotion. Emotions are not, as traditional theories suggest, triggered by events we encounter. They are instead affected by our own, often idiosyncratic, *interpretations* of events. We also decide how we will feel, given our interpretations. Choice exists at several points. Our view of ourselves as helpless in the face of emotional onslaught simply does not fit the facts.

We judge what others feel in the same way we interpret ambiguity generally. There's nothing magical about the process. It's more difficult, but not different. Love is an especially interesting example. Our culture encourages us to search for love but defines it so it is practically impossible to find. In fact, culture affects the way we interpret in a wide variety of situations. By affecting our readiness to see some things and not others, our culture plays a decided role in what we see, when, and how we feel about it. Culture also pressures us to feel "appropriately."

In short, new research in perception and learning turns our view of ourselves upside down. In conventional views, we are passive. Early events shape our personalities, our motives, and our emotions. The primary impact of culture occurs in our formative years, during which we internalize its values (in the Freudian tradition) or become subject to its reinforcements (in the behaviorist). Later life is seen as a playing out of early psychological scripts, or reinforcement schedules.

In the new view, we are active. Our theories *in the present* affect perception, learning, and emotion. The way we interpret affects what we see, and how we feel. Culture operates in the present to influence, but cannot control, our interpretations. Most important, our interpretations are self-fulfilling.

The first part of the book shows why *what we see always seems to fit our theories*. The second part of the book, which deals with interaction, shows how *we influence each other's theory making, and behavior, in ways which are self-fulfilling.* It is this active self-fulfilling aspect of interpretation and interaction that sets Constructive Psychology apart. Rather than play out minor variations of predetermined scripts, Constructive Psychology sees us creating at every instance our ongoing, and changing, social reality.

Like Zeno's arrow that cannot possibly get from one place to another because it must go through an infinity of points to get there, clear communication and unambiguous interaction is "impossible." People see things differently—and always will. In addition, the way we talk militates against our noticing these differences.

Ironically, though we see things differently, and cannot know what others see, we influence each other's views. The influences work so that people often behave in exactly the way others expect. We rise and fall to each other's expectations. The same thing happens in groups. Problems that two people have talking are multiplied by the number of people present. In groups, things get better or worse faster.

Final chapters of this book deal with implications. "Fast Change" debunks the magic of therapies in our culture. When they work, which is not often enough, they are effective because they recognize the ambiguity with which we deal and suggest alternative explanations. The interpretations they suggest need not be correct.

In chapter 13, "Truth and Consequences," the significance of Constructive Psychology is discussed. The research suggests we have far more freedom, and responsibility, than we generally credit. We can and do influence the course of social interaction.

Let me expand this point. Constructive Psychology shows that people actually make choices and have responsibility for their actions, even when they do not know they do. In contrast, older theories suggest we are: 1) driven by unconscious impulses (either sexual or aggressive) over which we have little if any influence, or are, 2) controlled by environmental contingencies which we are relatively helpless to counteract. But recognizing that we have responsibility increases the chance we will take it; acknowledging we are able to make choices increases the likelihood we will make them wisely. Changing the way we view ourselves would revolutionize the way we lead our lives and maintain our relationships.

I use the term revolution deliberately. Changes in scientific theories, the way scientists view the world, often result in revolutions of thought.[1] The Copernican revolution, the change from seeing the earth as the center of the universe, is one such switch. It affects our theology, our values, the way we live and treat each other from day to day. The impact of such revolutions is hard to predict.

Interestingly, recent developments in particle physics suggest where the revolution in psychology might lead. I say this because physics itself underwent a revolution which closely parallels developments in psychology.

Historically, physicists thought technology would lead to a single, factual, understanding of the physical world. But physicists find they never reach the "truth." What they see is always affected by the tools they use— and cannot help but be. The "reality" of an object seen through the naked eye, an X-ray, or a microscope, varies; one is no truer than another. Similarly, the new psychology shows that objective reality *cannot* be perceived. People see and act differently because they interpret events. Their differences are not aberrations (due to early traumas or reinforcement schedules) but unavoidable diversities in interpretation, in the present. Some interpretations work better than others—whether or not they are "correct." (The betterness of some interpretations is discussed in chapters 9, 10, and 11.)

Secondly, physicists find they must live with "uncertainty": small particles do not behave in predictable fashions. They change rapidly from what we generally consider energy to what we generally consider mass. Their direction and speed cannot be anticipated. While scientists can predict how, on the average, a group of particles will behave, they cannot predict the behavior of particular particles. This contradicts the view of classical physics which assumes the universe is predictable and blames failures of prediction on poor technology. Ironically, better technology has led physicists to conclude they must give up on prediction and rely on probability.

The problem is analogous to the psychologist who wants to study crowds. He can predict with reasonable accuracy what the crowd will do in different situations. He is unable to predict how any one individual will respond. Until recently, psychologists assumed that their failure to predict individual behavior reflected a failure of their science. Many still believe that is so. But the new psychology suggests that prediction in individual cases will always be impossible, a position I find comforting.[2]

In any event, the powerful similarity of theories arising from fields as diverse as psychology and particle physics is striking. The old-fashioned physicist tried to find out what matter is "really" like. Traditional psychologists spend inordinate time trying to determine what others "really" think, feel, or want. Ironically, the attempt to find "real" answers is as futile for psychologists as for physicists. As this book shows, what people see and do will always be affected by choices they make, by their early interpretations and their readiness to see—the tools they bring to situations. Acceptance of psychological relativity and uncertainty will be revolutionary.

For several years, physicists have been groping for a value system that meshes with their new world view; a world without certainty needs updated guidelines regarding choice, freedom, and responsibility. The new psychology requires similar guidelines. Like the Copernican revolution, understanding Constructive Psychology entails a shift in many of our culture's basic assumptions.

Interestingly, the increasingly popular literature on consciousness meshes well with new views in psychology (and physics)[3] and offers it a congruent value system. (The strengths and weaknesses of such a system are discussed in chapter 13.) Consciousness simply means awareness. And changes in consciousness are what this book is about. The assumption that we cannot know reality is itself a major change of consciousness, and it leads us to see, hear, and feel the world differently. It forces a choice between letting go or maintaining our attachment to certainty, a certainty that is not attainable. In fact, letting go of certainty and accepting ambiguity is exactly what Eastern students of consciousness mean by "nonattachment." If Buddha had not, modern psychologists would eventually have had to coin the term.

The ideas presented in this book are not complex and are not difficult to understand. I have written for readers without any background in psychology. At the same time, students of psychology, sociology, and consciousness will find my use of theory, and my conclusions, interesting. Notes are included for those who want references to studies cited and suggestions for further reading. I have also used notes when related ideas would have interrupted the flow of the text but seemed worth including in supplemental form.

Despite their simplicity, the ideas in this book present a view of the world signally and powerfully different from the view now held. The anecdotes and examples are commonplace—they are concerned with nothing more nor less than daily life. But the way we see ourselves day to day and the way we live are forcefully affected by the assumptions we bring to the events we encounter.

Constructive Psychology sees people as active rather than passive, as creators rather than responders, as actors —not merely as creatures acted upon. That change in perspective, a change of consciousness, alters our view of the world. Its impact is enormous.[4]

*WHY DON'T YOU
LISTEN TO
WHAT I'M NOT SAYING?*

part

I

INDIVIDUALS
AND
AMBIGUITY

1

I Wonder What
He Meant by That

Two psychiatrists pass each other on the street.

First psychiatrist:	"Good morning."
Second psychiatrist (to himself):	"I wonder what he meant by that."
Professor Craig:	"Good morning, sir. How are you?"
Professor Einstein:	"Relative to what?"

Until recently, psychologists assumed that social interaction was based on perception, perception that was more or less accurate. Those of us who are "healthy," they argued, perceive accurately, while neurotics distort reality. The extent of perceptual distortion was, and still is by some, taken as a measure of neurosis.

The view that perception can and should be "accurate" has some interesting implications for daily life. We search for the true meaning of actions, and analyze our own thoughts to find out what we really mean, really feel, or really want. We blame ourselves for perceiving inaccurately. We work hard to improve accuracy on the unfounded assumption that accuracy is attainable and will alleviate our problems. We fight with each other endlessly over whose perception is correct.

The view that perception can and should be accurate permeates our culture. It is a simple view—and inaccurate. New research (discussed in later chapters) shows that "perception" is always interpretation. Normals and neurotics differ not in the accuracy of their perceptions, but in the effectiveness of their interpretations. We all interpret all of the time. The way we interpret determines how the world looks, and whether we get through the day smoothly. Effectiveness, not accuracy, is what counts. Our interpretations always look accurate; they don't always look effective.

Social interaction involves interpretation. If our mate slams the door on entering the house, we may guess something is the matter, and may even guess what is the matter, although we do not know for sure. In a similar fashion, our children's tendency to avoid going to bed at night, or a friend's failure to phone over the last several weeks, or our boss's habit of scowling when we enter the office may all have significance. But often, we do not know what the significance may be.

Interpretation is complicated because it is difficult to clarify ambiguity. We cannot always ask people why they scowl, or why they have not phoned. Sometimes, we do not ask because we think it would be rude. Asking more often would help, but even if we ask, the ambiguity remains.

Consider Fran and Benito Biernat, a couple in their late thirties. They have been married eight years. Fran's son, Jason, who is now fifteen, lives with them. Though they do not notice, the three of them interpret ambiguity throughout the day.

Fran has just come home from the office. Ten minutes later Benito gets in. He slams the door and thumps to the bedroom. Fran interprets his behavior; she cannot act until she does. If she thinks he is angry about last night's fight she acts one way; if she thinks he got tied up in traffic, another.

Even if Fran asks what is wrong, she may not believe the answer she gets. She thinks Benito is angry. Responses like "I didn't slam the door" or "It was hard to close it with my hands full" will not be convincing. She closes the door with her hands full; there must be something else. She will try to figure out what's really happening.

The words "really happening" suggest there is "really" only one thing happening, that she can reach the truth if she searches hard enough and asks the right questions. That is *not* so. Benito might have slammed the door because he was angry (at Fran, at his boss, or the traffic conditions) or frustrated. Probably several factors contributed to his action.

The words "really happening" also suggest that *he* knows why he slammed the door. He may not. Very likely he was not aware of his reasons, or was aware of one but not all of the reasons involved. He may not even know he slammed it. When he tells her he did not, he may not be lying. Whether he is lying, like the reason he slammed the door, can't be determined.

Fran interprets events by *generating and testing theories*. She wonders whether Benito is angry, whether he had a bad day at the office, encountered heavy traffic, or slipped on the unshoveled driveway. If his hands are empty, his face scowling, and he answers her questions with a curt "Goddammit, can't I have a few moments quiet?" her theory that something is wrong seems substantiated.

The same thing happens all the time. If Fran and Benito suddenly stop nagging Jason about where he is going, with whom, and for how long, he is likely to notice the change. He will try to figure out what happened. Perhaps they have seen how mature he is and decided to leave him alone; they realize he can be trusted. Alternatively, they may have given up in despair and no longer care what happens. He will test these theories. If neither fits, he will think of others until he finds one that does. At that point, ambiguity will seem resolved.

But several explanations are likely to fit. Because behavior is ambiguous, Jason's assumption that his parents trust him *and* his assumption that they've given up will mesh with their behavior. They no longer nag him, and give him greater freedom. He could settle for either view.

In fact, the conclusion Jason draws about their actions has little to do with what is happening. His parents may have stopped nagging for reasons he'll never suspect. They may be too busy fighting to notice when he gets home. He notices only the change in their relationship to him, and not to each other. He sees the world through his own theories.

Jason's conclusion influences his response. If he thinks that they see him as mature, he is likely to gain self-confidence, treat them in a friendly manner, and show appreciation of their new respect. If he thinks they have given up on him, he might sulk around the house, become less communicative, and stay out later than ever.

In effect, he creates a social reality. It makes no difference whether his parents respect him, despair of him, or are having problems of their own. His interpretation determines his responses.

In the same way Benito, who wonders why Fran has bought several new dresses and four pairs of shoes after years of wearing old slacks and loafers, considers several explanations. If she just received a large pay raise he might think the added money explains her purchases. If she is worried about her fortieth birthday and talks about getting older he may make different assumptions. Alternatively, he may think she is having an affair with the well-dressed man who moved next door.

If he concludes that Fran is having an affair, his chance of finding evidence to the contrary is, to say the least, minimal. The likelihood of finding "evidence" that supports his assumption is great. She came home from work late last Wednesday, was not in her office Thursday morning when he phoned, and has suddenly started "playing bridge" on Thursday nights. The truth of the matter, that she hit traffic Wednesday, went shopping Thursday, and actually plays bridge on Thursday evenings is likely to stay hidden from him and, except for the bridge game, cannot be verified. If convinced she is cheating, he might even assume that Fran's friends lie about the bridge game.

Thinking that Fran has been unfaithful, Benito might himself have an affair, behave differently toward her, or behave differently toward his neighbor. If he thinks she is buying clothes because she's depressed he may become more supportive, might encourage her outside activities, or invite the neighbor whom she seems to find interesting in for coffee. His conclusions influence his actions. He creates a social reality.[1]

MAKING MEANING

The world we live in is affected by our interpretations. The view that reality exists independent of interpretation is false. Though events we interpret are commonplace, even trivial, the creation of social reality is not. The way we respond to "trivial" events determines how we feel about our friends, our jobs, and our families. The reality we create when we interpret ambiguity is, for better or worse, the one we live with.

The same thing happens in what we generally consider more important contexts, in financial or political circles. Actions that in themselves seem trivial—who sits next to whom or the shape of a negotiating table—are interpreted and often have important consequences. In fact, we are accustomed to recognizing the importance of "trivia" in politics. Columnists write pages analyzing the significance of a handshake, the elegance of a state dinner, and the form of address used in official greetings. The course of history is affected by interpretations given to such events and we do not take them lightly. In view of this, it is interesting that we fail to recognize the role of ambiguity in daily life or to recognize how interpretations we make affect the course of our own actions.

Imagine a film in which Jason Biernat is the central character. In fact, two or more films are possible. In one the audience is told and sees that Fran and Benito are worried about finances. Jason interprets the change in their behavior as the development of trust. He changes from a morose, unhappy youth to a self-confident young man who falls in love with the lovely girl next door. In this version, his misunderstanding forms the basis for comedy. In an alternative script, the audience knows his parents are worried about finances but Jason interprets the change in their behavior as rejection. He becomes withdrawn, his school work suffers, and he starts hanging out with the hoodlum next door. If carried to extreme, this stereotypic drama becomes a stereotypic tragedy.

Ironically, we live our lives like Jason, unaware of many choices that we make and oblivious to their significance. Because we are not aware that we interpret (what we hear, see, and feel seems determined by events) we are not aware of the options we ignore and the decisions that we make. But seeing the comedy and drama in Jason's life hinges on an awareness of ambiguity and choice. Recognizing, directing, and appreciating the comedy and drama in our own lives requires a similar recognition of choice. We do make meaning and, like fictional characters of stage and screen, the meaning we make is the reality we know.

The view of people as meaning makers is relatively new to psychology. It grows from studies of human development, perception, and information processing. The intriguing aspect of this research is the emphasis it places on us as theory makers, as a genuine force in the shaping of our own lives. We become both scientists testing theories and writers constructing visions of the world we inhabit and, where possible, share with others. For this reason I call the view presented in this book "Constructive Psychology." It describes how we construe and virtually build the world we inhabit. Later chapters show why the view is constructive, in the sense of helpful. Knowing we are theorists who interpret events can help us interpret, and act, in ways that are effective.

But we don't make theories in a vacuum. Our theory making is influenced by real people and real events which we encounter. Just as the steps that we as dancers make traversing the dance floor are partly a function of what we each feel like doing at any particular moment, our partner's movements, and what we each think our partner might be doing, so our social interaction is a kind of social dance—each partner influencing and being influenced by the other.

The dance analogy is apt. We live on relatively large and sometimes crowded dance floors, with the patterns (and sometimes the partners) changing. The changes are constant. The movements we make and the stories we tell about the dance are influenced by the music we hear, our own desires, and by the others on the floor—the patterns of space and movement created by those around us.

This book is about that dance—what the dance feels like, how we choose the steps, how the steps we choose influence other dancers and our partners. Interestingly, the view that we are dancing with others (not fighting against or walking beside them) influences the dance we do, who we dance with, whether or not we trip, and whether we enjoy the music.

2

The Child Is
Father to the Man

The view that we are writer/dancers who interpret
events comes from research on child development. That
research contradicts Freudian and behaviorist assumptions that what we learn is determined by events we encounter—what is really happening. Within those traditional frameworks, early experience is important because
we learn from objective events. Inaccurate perceivers also
learn from the events they encounter; what they learn is
distorted and not very functional. Therapy in these
frameworks consists of correcting old distorted learnings
based on inaccurate perception or inappropriate reinforcement. The assumption that reality is perceived, not
interpreted, permeates these views. They present a picture of human beings who are shaped (more or less well)
by objective reality—early childhood experiences or reinforcements, depending on the theorist's orientation.

In contrast, new research shows that past experiences are not what they seem. Because we interpret
events, *our early experiences are shaped by our own interpretations*. That explains why some people who seem

terribly deprived to observers mature beautifully, and others who seem to "have everything" display characteristics observers associate with deprivation. It is not the events themselves but our interpretation of events that is important. In turn, these early interpretations shape our understanding of later events.

How We Learn

As children we begin developing concepts, sometimes called schemas, that define the categories of our world: breast, mother, blanket, toy. When events fit our schemas, we recognize them as instances of the relevant category. When they fail to fit, we usually take a closer look and modify our concepts to accommodate discrepant events.[1] New schemas are formed by these changes.

Consider the development of an early concept—breast. At first the infant senses pressure to his lips and eventually develops a schema he codes "pressure on lips." After a while he recognizes "one of those" when the pressure reappears. A relatively simple concept has been formed. In a short time, the child learns that sucking "it" releases a liquid. It is "one of those" if (1) it presents appropriate pressure and (2) sucking releases a liquid.

Assuming that these criteria do define breasts, we can see why a baby sometimes refuses to feed. If the nipple doesn't feel right it's obviously not a breast, why suck on it? For a bottle-fed baby, the color of the bottle or the shape of the nipple becomes a defining criteria and, much to his parents' dismay, no substitutes which differ on these dimensions are accepted. He responds not to the bottle, but his theory about bottles.[2]

A child develops many concepts at once and gradually learns how they relate. He might, for example, have developed independent concepts about breasts and being held. With time he may link the two in a theory: "When I get held, breasts come." Alternatively the child may first develop a global concept in which breasts and being held are linked: "The breast holds me." Eventually, he encounters misfits from this global schema and revises his concepts to fit the new events.

Dealing with Ambiguity. A problem arises when events are more ambiguous. Mother looks "grumpy." Is she angry, frustrated, or tired? The cues that define expressions, unlike cues that define breasts, are not so clearly specified.

Sometimes context helps. Mother is usually angry when something spills—did something spill? She's usually tired when she's been working—has she been working? But even answers to these questions do not insure that he codes correctly.

Specific rules describe how he handles ambiguous events. He searches *until he finds a category that fits*. The search stops when one is found; the object is coded. Given an "angry or tired mother," he will code in whichever category he tries first.[3]

Imagine eight-year-old Susan playing in the park. She shouts hello to Bill, who does not answer; either he didn't hear or doesn't want to play. Her perception affects what she does. If she thinks he didn't hear she might continue shouting. Or she might get angry.

Susan is likely to find validation for *whichever view she takes*. If she catches his attention and he wants to play, he will be friendly. If he wants to be alone he may tell her so or, more likely, pretend he did not hear—a response that fits with adult etiquette. In that case, her assumption that he did not hear would seem confirmed—though she is wrong.

If Susan thinks he does not want to play and does

not approach him, *she cannot find she's wrong*—though she may be. If she then acts aggressively, he is likely to get angry. This will confirm her theory about rejection and *make it more accessible.*

What Susan learns depends as much on her assumptions as on events themselves. In turn, what she learns influences what she sees in future situations by making some categories, those she uses frequently, more readily available than others. Susan usually makes category decisions so fast she isn't aware she does it. For that reason, she is usually unaware of ambiguity. Once she codes an event it does not seem ambiguous.

WHAT WE LEARN

Because most events are ambiguous, our habitual ways of seeing *seem* to be accurate. Our perceptions appear to be valid. As the number of our categories grow, instances that do not fit become fewer and fewer. That doesn't mean perceptions get more accurate—only that, with many categories, finding one that fits is easy. Because existing categories fit, we rarely develop new categories or alter readiness. Early schemas often go unchanged. For this reason, our *early constructs often influence later interpretations.*

Learning About Oneself. A child learns about himself in the same way he learns about other things. His own behavior and the way people treat him (including words, vocal inflection, and body language) convey information about what he does, what he is supposed to do, and how what he does is valued.

The way Jesse evaluates his competence is a good example of how the process works and the way it influences future action. Because competency cannot be evaluated in isolation, Jesse must compare himself to others. Even concrete skills, like building castles, shooting baskets, or getting home runs, are difficult to evaluate in the absence of feedback. Jesse can shoot eight out of ten baskets. But it's not the score alone that counts. Does he shoot well, or do most children his age get ten baskets at a similar distance? He considers his performance in relation to his peers and, on the basis of that information, draws conclusions about his competency.

Jesse's theories about himself serve in the same way as theories about objects—they form the basis of his expectations. The decision that he plays quite well suggests he will play well in the future[4] and leads him to play rather than avoid games.[5] He is likely to play more often than Barbara, who thinks that she plays badly. So he gets more practice than she, and continues to improve. Barbara, who thinks she plays poorly, avoids playing and starts to look worse as Jesse's game gets better. *Their theories are self-fulfilling.*

Intellectual development is the same. Expectations of success or failure strongly influence performance in predictable ways. A now classic study by Robert Rosenthal[6] powerfully illustrates the way in which learning about themselves influences children's behavior. Rosenthal gave a group intelligence test to all the children in a public elementary school. He pretended it predicted which children would show improved academic ability. Teachers were then given the names of a few children who would blossom during the year. These children were no different from others in the class. Nonetheless, by the end of the year children in grades 1 and 2 who were "expected" to improve showed significant gains in IQ scores compared to other children. Apparently teachers' expectations affected the way they acted toward these children.[7] In turn, the change in their teachers' behavior led the children to alter their theories about themselves. The change in their theories affected their behavior.

The Rosenthal study is dramatic, and especially relevant in our culture where academic success is valued. But more important, the dynamics this study illustrates, operate in a variety of circumstances, not just in school. Children's *interpretations,* their theories about what is happening, have dramatic affects. The test children in Rosenthal's study *became better students.* That they "really" weren't late bloomers is irrelevant; in the environment Rosenthal created, they really were.

Learning About Relationships. In making meaning, children use, as much as possible, all available data—who speaks, to whom, in what tone of voice, and in what circumstances. A snippet of family dialogue shows a wealth of information can be culled from one short sentence.

Imagine a family of four at their dinner table. The father asks his daughter Sarah (age 10) to "help Mother and get some milk for Dave (age 3)." What might David learn from this event?

To begin, it appears that Mother is in charge of getting milk. The father didn't say, "Help *me* and get milk for Dave." Dave might infer that ten-year-olds are old enough to help, and are supposed to; three-year-olds probably aren't or he'd have been asked to help. Alternatively, Dave might guess women are in charge of milk. Perhaps three-year-olds are old enough to get some things but only women get milk. He'll check that out later.

Now imagine the same family with the addition of Mark (age 11). Father again asks Sarah to "help Mother and get some milk for Dave." If Dave had thought Sarah was asked because she was oldest, the presence of Mark who is older might lead Dave to think sex is critical. Alternatively, he might assume Father prefers Sarah over

Mark, or Mark over Sarah, depending on whether he thinks getting the milk is a chore or an honor.

Mark's presence alters Dave's theory; age isn't the answer. He may not know what is, but he knows it isn't age alone. Mark doesn't have to say anything to affect Dave's thinking. The fact that he does not say anything (like "I'll get it" or "Go get it yourself, Dad" or "Please, can't I get it for a change") is itself instructive.

Of course children, like adults, do not build theoretical empires in a day. We do not assume we know someone well (that we understand his theories) after one meeting, and Dave does not develop theories from only one remark or an hour at the table. Instead, each encounter is considered against the background of his experience. If the interaction is typical, it is likely incorporated and no change occurs in his theoretical system. If it differs from Dave's view, if Dad's remark or a negative reply from Sarah violates his expectations, he will attend to that difference and, if necessary, revise his theories.

If Sarah says, "Who are you to boss me around!" Dave may reconsider who is in charge, wonder if Sarah is naughty, wonder if Sarah is sick, or wonder if he heard her correctly.

Dave's father has the same set of options. What he actually says sheds light on the way he interprets. Few of us would be surprised by any of the following responses:

"I am your father, now get the milk."
"Don't talk back."
"What did you say, young lady?"
"Who do you think you're talking to?"
"She's not feeling well."

Everyone at the table will learn a great deal from whichever response he makes.[8]

Ironically, his father's response helps Dave decide what's happening. It will help him resolve the ambiguity and in doing so influences the way he revises his theory. Next time Sarah talks back her behavior will not seem ambiguous. Dave may not be right but in future he will "know" what is happening. As an adult dealing with his own children Dave will "know" why daughters talk back. Years later his response to his daughter will reflect that knowledge.

Dave is also constructing theories about what it means to be male or female, a son or daughter, a husband or wife. Had her father told Sarah that "girls should help their mothers," it would be quite clear he doesn't think boys need do so. No one has actually to do anything— words are enough. If Mark offers to get the milk, or gets up to get it, Dave will make meaning from Mark's action (boys *can* help but need not) and from his parents' response to that action.

Unfortunately, studies of sex role behavior in both homes and offices show that actual change in recent years has not been great. As a result, children today, like children of previous generations, are learning a variety of sex role stereotypes from what they hear and see. Even when both parents work, the nature of the work they do, the seriousness, respect, and status with which that work is treated, as well as who does the cooking and child-care after work, are still strongly determined by sex. Working women hold less prestigious jobs than men. They also do 75 percent of household tasks despite their full-time working status.

If after work, parents alternate cooking and cleaning, who does which seems irrelevant to sex. Children in such families learn more about sharing than what it means to be male or female. If mother always cooks and father does the clean-up, children probably learn that women cook and men do clean-ups.

How parents talk about what they do is often as important as how they do it. Language offers information that action alone does not. Sandra and Daryl Bem suggest the test of reversibility for people who want to find out about nonconscious assumptions hidden in language.[9] For our enlightenment, they present the following description of a modern marriage:

> *Both my wife and I earned Ph.D. degrees in our respective disciplines. I turned down a superior academic post in Oregon and accepted a slightly less desirable position in New York where my wife could obtain a part-time teaching job and do research at one of the several other colleges in the area. Although I would have preferred to live in a suburb, we purchased a home near my wife's college so that she could have an office at home where she would be when the children returned from school. Because my wife earns a good salary, she can easily afford to pay a maid to do her major household chores. My wife and I share all other tasks around the house equally. For example, she cooks the meals, but I do the laundry for her and help her with many of her other household tasks.*

Now this version:

> *Both my husband and I earned Ph.D. degrees in our respective disciplines. I turned down a superior academic post in Oregon and accepted a slightly less desirable position in New York where my husband could obtain a part-time teaching job and do research at one of the several other colleges in the area. Although I would have preferred to live in a suburb, we purchased a home near my husband's college so that he could have an office at*

home where he would be when the children re-
turned from school. Because my husband earns a
good salary, he can easily afford to pay a maid to
do his major household chores. My husband and I
share all other tasks around the house equally. For
example, he cooks the meals, but I do the laundry
for him and help him with many of his other
household tasks.

As the Bems point out, it seems unlikely that many men or women would see the second marriage as equalitarian or desirable. In our culture the husband looks too accommodating, the wife overbearing.

In any event, children learn what is appropriate and desirable for men and women by listening as well as watching. Their theories about what it means to be male or female influence how they think about themselves, how they respond to males and females generally, how they expect men and women to behave, and how they will respond if they fail to do so.

Our early constructs, often primitive and distorted views of complex interactions, cast a strong and pervasive influence over later perception and action. What we learn, as children or as adults, depends on assumptions we bring to events we encounter. The old view, that what we learn depends on events *per se,* simply does not hold. Rather, the assumptions we bring to early events affect our experiences of them in ways which are usually self-fulfilling and influence later interpretation.

3

Ready, Get Set, See

We interpret events in terms of existing, and often outdated, concepts. These are the only ones available to us. *The assumption that we do (or can) see objectively is false.*[1] Even the perception of size is affected by individual differences. As one relatively early study shows, poor children see coins larger than their middle-class counterparts, and that difference increases with the coins' value. Both groups of children judged coins to be larger than cardboard discs of equivalent sizes.[2] Even when we think we see the same things (a coin) we do not. What we see is *always* affected by who we are. Further, research shows that specific variables affect why we see things differently.

Many studies show that "perception" is constructed. In one, a group of subjects were shown a deck of playing cards in which color and suit were inappropriately matched (a red six of spades).[3] The cards were flashed very quickly on a screen and subjects were asked what they saw. Almost no one saw the cards correctly. A red six of spades was often seen as a black six of spades or a red six of hearts. Some subjects even saw a purple six of spades, apparently compromising their readiness to see spades in black with the actual red presented.

In fact, a variety of factors influence perception. They affect the order in which we generate theories and what we see in any given situation.[4]

Frequency. In ambiguous situations, we see what *usually* happens, not necessarily what *is* happening. And life is usually ambiguous. While psychologists must resort to flashing pictures at subjects to create artificial ambiguity, the real world presents most of us with more ambiguity than we generally need.

Several studies illustrate the effect of frequency. They also illustrate how even psychologists' theory making can be wrong. In 1949, a researcher named Elliott McGinnies[5] set out to illustrate the concept of denial put forward by Freud. With the aid of a tachistoscope (a slide projector capable of flashing pictures for exact split-second intervals) he presented subjects with a long list of words. The words were initially presented so quickly it was impossible to read any of them. But the list was repeated many times and at each repetition the exposure time was increased. McGinnies recorded the length of exposure necessary for particular words to be correctly identified by the student subjects, who were asked to write them down as soon as they thought they knew what a word said.

McGinnies was interested in denial and wanted to prove that people willfully refuse to see things that upset them. So his list consisted of some quite ordinary words like apple, broom, dance, etc., and also some that he thought would be resisted by his viewing audience, words like penis, Kotex, and whore. (In the unofficial annals of psychology this is called the "dirty word study.") In any event, McGinnies' hypothesis seemed proven. It took more time for students to perceive the "dirty words" correctly and they made more errors before getting them correct. "Sex," for example, was often perceived as "six." It looked as if people repressed what they did not want to see. The problem for theorists was to figure out how subjects knew which words would offend them if they could not see the words first and how, if they saw the words first, they kept secret from themselves what they saw.

A later study by Richard Solomon and Davis Howes saved a lot of complex theorizing.[6] These men hypothesized that McGinnies' subjects did not repress the dirty words. They pointed out that dirty words are not frequently seen in print (it was 1949). Subjects would not be expecting dirty words and might be embarrassed to say they recognized a dirty word if they were not sure. After all, they argued, it's not embarrassing to say that "sex" is "six" if you are not sure what it says, but it sure looks odd to identify the word "six" as saying "sex" when it does not. To test their theory, Solomon and Howes presented subjects with a list quite similar to McGinnies' and kept track of the frequency with which different words on their list appear in the English language. As they predicted, high frequency words were identified more easily (at faster exposure) than low frequency words. It appears that subjects run down the list of words in their heads that might fit the blur on the screen in an effort to match the blur with possible alternatives. Words that are more common are tried before uncommon words, and often appear to fit. The subject who sees "s x" on the screen in front of him is more likely, in running through the three-letter words he knows, to hit six before sex, and concludes that that is the word being flashed.

Of course, gynecologists might respond differently on this test from mathematicians or the general public.

And they do. Studies similar to these show that interests, professions, values, and personal background all affect frequency and hence what we perceive under ambiguous circumstances.

Frequency works to decrease the probability of noticing change when it occurs. If one child in a family usually spills food during dinner, her parents are likely to attribute the puddle of milk they discover to her—though in this case her sister might have had the spill. Conversely, if one child in a family is usually helpful, parents are likely to assume it was she who tidied the living room, though they do not know for sure. Frequency operates so we assume what usually happens is happening unless faced with clear evidence to the contrary.

Context. Another variable which affects accessibility is context.[7] We expect different things to happen in different locations and at different times. The word "s x" may read one way in a classroom, another in a bedroom. The word "l ve" looks different on a billboard showing a sexy couple sharing drinks than near a picture of a doctor administering emergency care. In the same vein, words spoken by a colleague at the office may not have the same meaning as the same words spoken at home by a mate, or at home by the colleague. The same words, in fact, may have different meanings when spoken by the same person, in the same location, but at different times.

Imagine a short conversation between husband and wife when both are in an excellent mood. They have just returned from a weekend vacation without the children.

W: It must be nice to be single and not have any responsibility.
H: I've thought of that also.
W: Of running away from it all?
H: How about you?

W: Of course. But I can't decide where I'd go.

H: I think I'd just bum on the beach with Frank for a while.

W: Well, send me a postcard when you get there. I'm going to bed now.

The same conversation after a fight would have an entirely different meaning. Even if delivered in the same tone of voice, the meaning might be altered if the husband suspected his wife of having an affair with their neighbor or if the wife thought her husband really did want to live with Frank.

Remarks like "I wonder why I married you," "I sure am lucky to have married you," or "We deserve each other" range in meaning from endearments to attacks depending on how they are heard. And how they are heard is largely a function of context.

Sequential Probability. A third factor which influences perceptual readiness is called sequential probability.[8] Though it has a fancy name, sequential probability is only slightly different from frequency and context. It reflects our learning about what usually occurs after some other event, independent of the overall frequency of the event or the specific context. Doorbells, for example, do not ring at my house with great frequency. And I usually do not find people just standing outside my door. Nonetheless, the probability of someone being there after the doorbell rings is high. In the same fashion, we expect thunder after lightning, kisses after hugs, and laughter after we tell our favorite joke. These expectations are instances of learned sequential probabilities. My expectation is caused by learning about the different probability of events after other events, as opposed to the probability of the event in general.

The fact that humans use sequential probability in

dealing with the world around them is one of the most intriguing results of research into information processing. Because we take it for granted that someone has rung the doorbell, or that some events are more likely than others at different times, the idea is commonplace. But it changes the way we understand interpersonal interaction.

We see things one way after one event, another way if they follow something else. It explains why we sometimes see what we expect to see when it has not happened, and hear what we expect to hear, when it has not been said. Those of us who have waited breathlessly for the words "I love you" on moonlit evenings and are then not sure we heard right when something like "I lumph you" is whispered in our ears, now understand why. Assuming our beloved really only murmured "I like you," what we have is a more emotional instance of the purple six of spades.

Sequential probability has its greatest effect when sequences of events occur with frequency. Then we begin to count on the second event fairly regularly following the first. In terms of other people and our perception of what they are doing, the longer we know a person the more chance we have of noticing such sequences, the more chance we have of perceiving their behavior to fit our expectations.

The first time I met Ron, I was surprised at how quickly he jumped from the table at the suggestion of a whimper from his four-week-old child. After several evenings at his home, I expected him to do so, and was surprised if he did not. On one occasion after hearing the baby cry and hearing someone go to the carriage, I assumed that Ron was, as usual, rocking the baby. He is much faster to respond than Mary. On that particular night I was wrong. What impressed me in retrospect was the certainty with which I knew who was rocking the child.

My friend Eva, for another example, usually gets quite tense in slow traffic. And being sensitive to her moods, I usually spend my time when with her in cars hoping traffic will move. I get increasingly tense when it does not because I know she will start fuming if it stops. The cycle was finally interrupted when Eva announced I was getting *her* nervous by fuming in traffic. She had been working hard not to get upset and insisted that she was no longer bothered by delays. When I stopped to check her appearance, it was obviously true. As I "knew" that she hates traffic, I had not needed to look.

Long-term relationships are filled with exactly that quality of "knowing." Sequential probability, a blessing which saves us from always wondering what's coming next, is at times too efficient. It is probability, not certainty.

We may "know" with fair certainty that our friends get nervous in traffic, do not like musical comedies, prefer cheesecake to pie, and would rather spend an evening with the Kleiners than two minutes with the Beckers. But even if we are 90 percent correct, one in ten times they will enjoy delays, go to musical comedies, order apple pie, and invite the Beckers to dinner. That is, if the probabilities do not change.

Additional room for error arises because people change. We develop new interests and new tastes. Our relatively set ways of responding are influenced by the people we meet, the events we encounter, the books which we read, and the television we watch. The probabilities concerning our behavior change over time. Eva used to read novels but now prefers nonfiction. She used to eat chocolate but now watches her weight. She used to be more politically conservative and then less conservative than she is now. People recognize her on the street after many years but she is not the same person.

Changes are even more common in children. The foods they once loved they often refuse to touch. The babying they once wanted is gradually rejected. They behave differently over time and demand we behave differently in dealing with them.

But *our readiness to see what we expect militates against our noticing change*. We do not alter our theories until the differences from what we expect are overwhelming. Then we can no longer fit the data to our theories.

The first time my child announces he does not like the person I consider his best friend, I assume they have had a fight. A few days later when his friend is over, I hear them bickering; I assume they are tired and cranky. When a week goes by and the friend has not stopped by, I assume he is busy with school work. When he does knock on the door and my son refuses to play, I assume *he* is busy. I also assume they play when I am not around. It is easy for me to persist in believing that the boy down the street, with whom my son has not played for the last several weeks and has not considered a friend for even longer, is his best friend, the one he yearns to see. It's no wonder I get funny looks at the end of two months' time when I finally wonder out loud about not seeing what's-his-name for the last few days. It is even worse when I greet the news that they are not friends with a surprised and maternal, "But you like him so much."

A CONSTRUCTIVE ATTITUDE

Understanding that perception always entails interpretation changes the way we treat differences in perception. The traditional assumption that one interpretation is right and another wrong often leads to frustration and, at times, disagreement and resentment. We argue over what has really happened, what was really said or really meant. Later we argue when we recall events, because one of us remembers wrong. Even some psychiatrists of the old school help us remember our past in an effort to understand the present, forgetting that the past was itself a construction.

In the Constructive view differences in interpretation reflect honest differences, not errors. We can rarely say with certainty that one person is wrong and the other right. Differences understood in this way are more acceptable (we can agree to disagree) and, to greater or lesser extent, unavoidable. Even when we seem to agree about something—that it is a coin, for example— we probably perceive it differently.

4

Feel This[1]

Nᴇᴡ research also challenges traditional thinking about emotion. It refutes the traditional view that emotions are passively triggered by objective events; in the established view, events control our emotions. When things go well, when what we want is actually happening, we feel good. When people laugh at our jokes, appreciate our wit, recognize our brilliance, and give us the gifts we want, we feel happy, not sad. When everything goes wrong, when our jokes and our soufflés fall flat, the job we want falls through, and the relationships we crave fall apart, we feel sad, not happy.

But events in themselves are not good or bad, happy or sad. We interpret events. We make meaning from ambiguity and decide what is happening. *We respond emotionally to interpretations, not to events as such.*

Interpretation seems irrelevant when things are unambiguous; did he or did he not burn the dinner? But important events are rarely so cut-and-dried. Whether our friends like us, or our mates love us, is more pressing. The answers to those questions are always ambiguous.

Mrs. Terry is a case in point. She came to me feeling insecure and unappreciated after fifteen years of marriage. Her husband hardly talked to her, didn't seem to listen to her, and behaved in general as if he wasn't there. She didn't think he was anywhere else in particular, but that was little consolation. The morning of her thirty-fifth birthday, he gave her an espresso coffee maker, something she wanted. The gift brought forth a flood of tears and new proof that he did not care. The gift was not obviously pleasing.

It turned out that Mrs. Terry wanted a particular kind of coffee maker, and her husband knew what kind she wanted. She took the fact that he bought a different kind as evidence he did not care. When he said he could not find the one she wanted, she took that to mean he did not care enough to look longer; he would spend half an hour to buy the right gift but not two hours if that's what was needed.

Her perception changed when he finally explained he *had* spent hours looking for the coffee maker she wanted, could not find it and, after much consideration, decided the one he got would do. Eventually Mrs. Terry was convinced he had understood and had tried to please her. She was also happy that he cared enough to comfort her and explain what had happened. As her interpretation changed, so did her feelings.

But differences between the traditional and new views of emotion go beyond interpretation to the question of attention. People pay attention to different aspects of events. Mrs. Terry focused on the coffee maker, not her other gifts. Another woman might not have given it a second thought. Attention is determined by expectations and interests, not objective events. The traditional view that events control emotion is wrong for two reasons. *Our own expectations, not events, determine what we notice in particular situations* and *how we interpret what we have noticed.* We respond emotionally to our interpretations.

DISCREPANCY INFLUENCES ATTENTION AND AROUSAL

Research shows *we focus on events which are different from our expectations.*[2] We do not pay attention to events that go exactly as we always knew they would. This has tremendous survival value. We need not dwell on all the events which occur on schedule. When something untoward happens, we notice it. Then we find out if it is something significant to which we must attend (the funny smell is the wastebasket on fire) or an innocuous event we can ignore (the funny smell is the man's after shave lotion). This very important survival mechanism has an interesting effect on us as social creatures: we notice error.

Because of the way we process information, we do not notice that the radio continues playing smoothly (though we notice static) or that our children and spouse come home on time (though we notice when they do not). We attend to the unexpected.

This means that different people notice different things. The husband whose wife has come home at six o'clock for the last seven years will know something is wrong when he gets home to find an empty house. The husband whose wife works late will know something is wrong when he gets home at five to find the table set and wine in the cooler. Each attends to what is different and tries to find out what is wrong.

"Wrong" does not mean anything is actually wrong. Both women might have inherited several thousand dollars—the first is still at the lawyer's, the second saw the lawyer that morning and took the day off work. "Wrong" only means different from expectation. Things seem initially "wrong" to the husbands.

We experience arousal (increases in blood pressure, muscle tension, and general metabolic rate) when things go "wrong."[3] If Louisa hears the doorbell ring, the fact that no one is there when she answers does not fit her expectation and she will experience surprise. Her arousal will increase. Her surprise is even greater if she opens the front door when the doorbell has *not* rung and someone *is* standing there. In that case she is even more likely to be surprised and will experience even more arousal. But these discrepancies are isolated. They bear no relation to other expectations.

If Louisa expects a long and happy married life and her husband comes home one night and announces he plans to leave her, the event is discrepant. It also threatens her expectations regarding life-style, financial security, emotional stability, and parenting. Its impact is not isolated. The greater the impact, the greater her arousal.

Consider Manuel, a happily married man who assumes that he will, and wants to, remain married. Discrepancy arises when his wife comes home one evening and announces, in suitably apologetic tones, that she has "fallen out of love" and is leaving him for another man. The husband has a wide range of emotional responses to choose from.

If he focuses on his wife or the other man as the cause of his arousal, he will respond with "anger." If he accepts her more fatalistic and passive description of events (she "fell out of love") and attributes no blame, he will feel sadness. If he focuses on what he has lost (wife, companionship), he feels grief. If he hopes she will return, he feels longing. If he focuses on the other man getting all he (Manuel) has lost, he feels envious. If he focuses on someone "seeing" him lose, he feels embarrassed.

The same series of choices exist in any number of situations. Imagine you have applied for a job which you thought you would get and find out that someone else was given the post. If you blame the personnel manager, you feel angry. If you assume that nothing would have helped, that the other person is better suited to the job than you, you feel disappointment. If you focus on what you have lost (a nice office, a raise in salary, and the company car), you feel sad. If you focus on the other person getting everything you lost, you feel envious. If you think the other person might refuse the job and focus on the off chance the job may still be yours, you feel hopeful. What you focus on determines how you label the arousal[4] and how you feel in any given instance. Past experience and readiness affect focus.

Positive emotions work in a similar way; arousal comes from discrepancies between what we want and what we perceive. But positive emotions entail a resolution of discrepancy. In positive emotion, the discrepancy has been eliminated. We feel happy.

On a commonsense level we know that feeling angry is different from feeling sad. And feeling happy is different than feeling excited. Amazingly, psychologists and physiologists have failed to find distinct physiological states that correlate with emotions. *Individuals* have consistent physical responses to particular emotions (some people feel anger in the throat, others in the stomach), but research does not show physiologically distinct emotion states that hold for all individuals.

Studies by Stanley Schachter in the 1950s show that physiologically unique emotion states are not needed to explain emotion.[5] In a series of studies he pretended to investigate the effects of vitamins on the nervous system.

He administered, to half his subjects, a stimulant that induces general physiological arousal. The other subjects, who also believed they were getting a shot of vitamins, received a placebo which had no physiological effect. Subjects were then put in a variety of situations and were asked to describe their emotional responses. Some subjects were asked to fill out a long, boring, and offensively personal questionnaire ("How many affairs has your mother had over the last few years?"). Others were shown comic or tragic movies and asked to rate the movies as an emotional experience. Others were taken to an amusement park and asked to rate the rides. In each situation, subjects who received the stimulant reported much stronger emotional responses than subjects who received the placebo.

Schachter's research supports the view that emotions reflect general physiological arousal, not unique physiological states. Once aroused, we look around in an effort to "explain" what happened and then label our arousal. Context alters readiness and offers one set of cues for labeling. In situations in which we are asked embarrassing and offensive questions, we are likely to label our arousal "anger," at tragedies we are likely to label our feelings "sad," and at funny movies and amusement parks as "happy."

A CHOICE OF FEELINGS

According to this theory, emotions are not what we generally imagine. Emotions do not arise passively.[6] *We play an active role in determining how we feel*. We focus on particular aspects of events. Then we interpret what we see *and* how we feel about it. Our interpretations and labels seem correct; we do not notice ambiguity.

What we do is influenced by the label we select. If angry we might fight, if sad we might cry, if depressed we might drink.

This does not mean we can decide to feel differently just because we want to. If we don't get the job or the invitation we want, it is foolish (and perhaps crazy) to work hard at feeling happy. If we want something and do not get it, the appropriate thing is to feel sad, or disappointed, not happy. Local mental hospitals are filled with people who laugh at sad events and cry when something lovely happens.

The choice lies at a different level. Our decisions about what we want and the number of events we arbitrarily make contingent upon them influence our emotions. It is one thing that Anna wants to be a lawyer. It is another for her to decide she can only be happy as a lawyer, cannot marry until she becomes a lawyer, and therefore cannot have the children she so badly wants if she does not get into law school. Assumptions like these increase the chance she will be disappointed in contrast to the assumption that acknowledges she would like to be a lawyer but could also do pretty well as an accountant, stock broker, or lab technician.

Similarly, the way she explains her failure if she doesn't get into law school will affect the way she feels. She can get angry at the fool who did not like her appearance (and ignored her high test scores), depressed because there is nothing she can do about her shortcomings, jealous because the woman down the street was accepted instead, or embarrassed because her friends knew she thought she'd get in and didn't.

Anna often responds with anger. When things go wrong she habitually checks the behavior of others to find out why. Because events are complex it is generally easy for her to blame others when events fail to meet her expectations. Whether Anna attributes their bungling to incompetence, carelessness, or malice is a matter of choice and will depend in part on context, in part on her readiness to consider these alternatives. In any case, because she looks first to the behavior of others in her effort to explain discrepancy, Anna often finds reasons to be angry. People who look to chance, or blame themselves first, never even notice the failures to which Anna is so sensitive.

If Anna does not get into law school, she will figure out why and fight to get in. If fighting fails, she will study hard to get in elsewhere. She will "show that idiot" she can do it. Her anger will lead to action. She is often successful because she is a fighter. Someone who is "prone to depression" would be more likely to withdraw.

Anna is not aware of her tendency to respond with anger in situations others perceive as disappointing. She is unaware of her tendency to always see a particular side of ambiguous events. But what she feels and how she responds is determined by where she looks and how she interprets what she sees. She is wrong when she thinks that events make her angry. Her theories about events, not events themselves, are critical.

5

Ah Love[1]

We also develop theories about other people's feelings. We test our theories by evaluating their actions. Jokes that suggest our loved ones would squeeze the toothpaste from the bottom of the tube "if they really loved us" reflect the way we often interpret behavior. The toothpaste joke is successful because it carries interpretation to an unusual extreme. The fact is, we do judge how people feel from the way they act, even if the act in question is trivial. Late arrivals, broken appointments, and messy toothpaste tubes are significant because of their symbolic, not their objective, meaning.

Unfortunately, we often fail to recognize the ambiguity upon which we base our evaluations of other people's feelings. Those perceptions are, like other perceptions, strongly influenced by our own past experiences and our readiness to interpret in habitual ways. Nonetheless, we allow them to have strong and often undue influence over us.

Consider love. The perception that someone loves

us affects the way we perceive what they do and influences decisions we make about them. Ironically, we use their behavior to determine how they feel about us and then allow our decision about how they feel to influence our perception of their behavior.

Because love is important in our culture, it is worth looking at how we recognize it. Like the infant figuring out if the ambiguous object is a breast, we develop criteria to determine whether other people (children, parents, spouses, or lovers) love us. Regardless of what love is, or whether it actually exists in any given instance, we test hypotheses and infer love from ambiguity.

A New Idea

Our culture's concern with love is relatively new. Prior to the twelfth century, the idea of romantic love was virtually nonexistent. It came to western culture not in the idealized version we now know but as ritual for the seduction of someone else's wife, by courtly lovers. Not until the seventeenth century was romantic love perceived as a valuable if not necessary aspect of daily living. Historians note that the family of the seventeenth century, like the families of the middle ages, did not generally provide affection—though affection may at times have existed. Neither the expression nor the perception of love was a necessary part of daily life.[2]

The following are typically described as components of romantic love: attention (the lover is absorbed in and attentive to the loved one); intimacy (the lover desires great intimacy—both physical and psychological—with the loved one); and generosity (the lover likes doing things for the loved one). The criteria necessary for the perception of love reflect these stereotypes.

Social scientists have, on the whole, given little attention to the issue of love.[3] A few have made theoretical statements about the value of love or investigated the effects of loving or lack of love on others. Some investigate which variables influence people falling or staying in love. The perception of love has been virtually ignored.

The failure of social science to deal with how one knows one is loved is interesting. Advertising has tried, and may well have succeeded in elevating the need to be loved (to perceive love) to unprecedented and discomforting heights. Research shows that 87 percent of male and 95 percent of female college students ranked "being loved" the most important need to be filled in love relationships.[4] Being loved has become both the means and the end. "Do you love me?" has become a very potent question.

THE CRITERIA

How do we know someone loves us?

The answer does not lie in specific behaviors. The behavior that signals love to one individual is often irrelevant to another. Secondly, behavior is ambiguous. The behavior we interpret as a show of love at one time will have different meanings at other times. The wife who interprets a gift of flowers as a show of love will probably interpret that gift differently after receiving a bouquet every Friday for six years, after a large and unresolved fight, after her spouse stumbles in late, or after she has developed an allergy to pollen. Flowers *per se* mean nothing.

What criteria do we use to determine when a behavior, any behavior, signifies love.

I. *Did I have to ask?*

No matter what the behavior, it will not be taken as love if we have to suggest the action. If, for example, a husband requests an elegant home-cooked dinner, and his wife cooks it, she will be seen as obedient, obliging, gracious, giving, or sacrificing depending upon his view, but not, in our society, as loving. Similarly, the woman who requests a particular gift and gets it (whether from a husband, lover, parent, or child) can infer a willingness to please—but not necessarily love.

In our culture people must love, and show love, "because they want to—not because they have been asked." But having been told "Do it because you want to, not because you've been told to," either a failure to do it or doing it because they have been told countervails the order. The more we need proof of love, the more we ask, the less satisfying the proof. If we ask, "Do you love me?", "Yes" will not be a satisfactory or proving answer. To "Yes" the unspoken reply is always "Prove it."

The need to show love without being asked is shown in the emphasis our culture places on remembering events like birthdays and anniversaries. To look loving it is more important to remember events than to do something about them. Imagine alternative scenes from a hypothetical movie. In Scene A, a husband at the office says to his secretary, "Today is my wife's birthday, and I'm in meetings all day. Would you buy her flowers?" In Scene B, the secretary reminds the husband that today is his wife's birthday and he says, "I'm in meetings all day. Would you buy her flowers?" In Scene C, the secretary reminds the husband it is his wife's birthday and he says, "I'm not in meetings today. I'll buy her flowers."

Given the lack of data, the viewer would conclude that husband A is most loving. Husband C gets little if any credit for having time to buy the gift, though his value as a boss might increase. We see the importance of remembering even more clearly when the husband in the above examples is exchanged for a working wife; imagine a woman forgetting her husband's birthday.

But let us leave the theater. It is only in movies that we know who remembered the event and who bought the gift. In real life, husbands simply come home with birthday presents. What wives think about who remembered depends on how the gift is presented, and their (the wives') theories and expectations about their husbands. What they think bears no direct relation to the facts.

II. *Do I like it?*

It is one thing to think that someone thought of doing something. It is another to judge their action appropriate and timely.

Errors of Time. If, for example, a woman especially likes eating in fine restaurants, a pastime her boyfriend can live without, she might feel loved when he, perhaps sensing she's depressed, suggests they go out for Chinese food. If, however, she is depressed because she's gained five pounds, and is two days into her latest diet, the situation changes radically. His dinner invitation under such circumstances would fail the "love" test. She usually wants to eat out but didn't when he asked. "Usually" doesn't count.

Errors of Choice. Alternatively, a failure to appear loving could arise (even though she likes to eat out, and wants to at the moment) because she hates Chinese food. If he doesn't know her preference in restaurants, the moment can be saved by a fast switch to steak. If, however, they've known each other long enough that she thinks he *should* know she doesn't like Chinese food, his suggestion is not likely to be taken as indicative of love. Quite the contrary.

Try another example: the stereotypical joke about the wife who buys her husband a tie he doesn't like. Assuming he gives her full credit for thinking of it—she was walking by the shop and "knew" he'd like it—it is still not worth anything symbolically. If it was the perfect tie it might show "love," but the wrong tie is worse than nothing. It is an object to elicit guilt and maybe even resentment. Especially if she's always bringing home clothes he doesn't like and he's asked her not to, her loving intentions are counterproductive. It doesn't look like love.

But why are we angered by the wrong gift? Partly because we don't know what to do with it. But the significance is deeper. It's as if the above husband were saying, "She knew I wouldn't like that tie!" And the wife above seems to say, "If you loved me, you'd know what I want." "If you loved me, you would read my mind!" In fact, knowing what to do and when to do it without being asked requires lovers to mind read if they want to look loving.

It is really quite a trick to appear loving or, from the loved one's point of view, to be loved. It requires that the lover know what the other wants, and when she or he wants it, without asking. Paradoxically, if the loved one becomes anxious about being loved, and asks for reassurance, it becomes even more difficult for the lover to look loving.

Husband: Do you love me?
  Wife: Yes. (Perhaps an honest response.)
Husband: You never show it.
  Wife: How can I show it? (A good question.)
Husband: You never _____ (e.g., say you love me, buy me presents, read my manuscripts . . .).

As we saw above, if the wife follows her husband's instructions she will not appear loving. She must "prove" love by a method he does not suggest. It requires great imagination and infinite versatility.

III. *Did you sacrifice?*

Compatibility. It looks as if it is easy for individuals to show love if they are compatible. If they like to spend leisure time in the same way, like to eat similar food, read similar books, have the same taste in clothes, movies, and friends, the probability of one initiating a behavior or making a suggestion that the other finds appropriate is great. And in fact the probability is greater as these similarities increase.

Unfortunately, love and compatibility are not the same in the romantic tradition. If your husband wants to play tennis when you want to play tennis, that is nice, and you are lucky, but it is no indication of whether he loves you. Something is missing.

That something seems to be sacrifice. If he suggests a game of tennis when you know he'd rather read, tennis looks like love. If there is nothing he would rather do than play tennis, tennis in no way reflects upon his feeling for you. The irony is obvious. The more compatible a couple, the easier it is to think of doing the right thing without being asked, the harder it becomes to look giving.

Cost. Failure to look loving arises from not only a lack of sacrifice due to compatibility but also lack of sacrifice defined simply as lack of cost (whether in money, time, or effort).

Interesting support for the cost hypothesis comes from developmental psychology. When asked how they know if their parents love them, adolescents reply (whether in the affirmative or negative) in terms of perceived cost, not gifts received. Children of wealthy parents dismiss gifts which can be bought and value gifts entailing time spent (playing together, or going to sports or entertainment events if it is time that is dear in the family). Conversely, children who receive gifts of time when time is plentiful, evaluate love on the dimension in short supply (usually money).[5]

Benefit. The criteria of sacrifice can also be violated by someone who "overly" enjoys sacrificing. If, for example, the loved one perceives (rightly or wrongly) that the lover is more concerned with proving he is a good husband, good father, or the most sacrificing person in town, the sacrifice criteria is violated because benefit accrues to the lover.[6] Accidentally accrued benefit is acceptable so long as it doesn't happen too often; then it begins to look intentional.

It is "sacrifice" that is usually in question when adolescent children accuse their parents of giving them the "best of everything" because the parents wanted to *for themselves*, or so they (the parents) would look good to neighbors. This is independent of whether the children themselves wanted the best of everything (new clothes, for example)—a question related to appropriateness.

The perception of generosity may be confused by the issue of appropriateness. It is possible to imagine parents who really did sacrifice, thinking the children wanted new clothes, though the parents didn't care. If the children did want the clothes and perceived the sacrifice, the parents would appear loving. If the parents misjudged and the children did not want clothing, the parents' poor choice might well suggest self-interest.

The reasoning goes: "If I don't want clothes, and they give me clothes, they must either think I want them (my parents don't understand me) or they wanted me to have them." Since "not understanding" precludes loving (how, after all, can someone be loved if they are not understood), it may be preferable to perceive selfishness than a lack of understanding.

It is practically impossible to look properly sacrificing, to seem motivated solely by the desire to please. Sacrifice acts as the test of love because the parents want to do something to please their children, not for themselves. If the children perceive that their parents enjoy sacrificing, the criteria is violated. The parents must appear to be doing something to please their children only because they want to, but must not appear to want to too much. If, on the other hand, the parents appear to suffer the sacrifice, they are not behaving in order to please the children. (How can the children be pleased if their parents keep complaining?) In order to look giving, the parents must convey that they want to do something for their children, would not be doing it except to please them, and are not overly enjoying pleasing them.

How does anyone manage to look loving? Return to the couple negotiating dinner. If he suggests Chinese food, which she at the moment finds attractive, he can convey either verbally ("I'd rather eat steak but . . .") or nonverbally (by the tone of voice or grimace) that Chinese food is not his first choice. It is obvious, however, that he cannot grimace all through the meal and still get credit for eating it. He must enjoy the meal with comments equivalent to "This is pretty good for Chinese food" or "I don't usually like Chinese food but . . ." If he gets very enthusiastic about the meal ("This is fantastic—I love Chinese food—from now on it's my favorite") he still gets credit for tonight, as he didn't know he'd like it when he came. But next time he suggests Chinese food, she will think he wants to go because it was so good last time. They are now compatible—but does he love her?

LOVE AS A HYPOTHESIS

The criteria described above are necessary for people to look loving but in no way assures that they will. If, for example, Pam and Keith are good friends, they may fulfill the above conditions which each one labels friendship. If, however, he suddenly finds her attractive and tries to determine whether she loves him, the conditions necessary for a positive reply are present.

There are, of course, individual differences between people which will affect the frequency with which each "looks for love" and the likelihood that each will find it independent of other people's behavior. Those who do not look, who do not test the relevant hypothesis, will not interpret behavior as loving. But seeking does not entail finding. Keith might assume that Pam is a dolt, incapable of an original idea, and assume that her best ideas, the things she does to please him, have been suggested by a friend. He might be difficult to please and rarely finds gifts satisfying. He might also be somewhat paranoid, attribute ulterior motives to people, and refuse to acknowledge sacrifice. Some people are harder to love, to show love to, than others.

Others find love everywhere. The smallest gesture may be seen as loving, as fulfilling the above criteria, by a sufficiently creative person. While for some a daily letter from a lover is inadequate, to others one postcard a month represents more than sufficient attention and sacrifice.

Needless to say, we do not test hypotheses about love in a vacuum. Our perception of any one instance is contaminated by our past interactions and expectations about others. If as a result of past instances we believe someone loves us, we are more likely to perceive the criteria as fulfilled than if we believe he or she is out for our money.

It is not necessary to perceive love all the time to think that someone loves us. It is only necessary to see it often enough. What we usually label love over an extended period of time are relatively few proving instances surrounded by ambiguous but congruent supportive data, instances in which one or two of the conditions are met. But ambiguous instances without proving instances are not sufficient, and enough will vary from individual to individual.

Love as defined by our culture is not easy to find. It is a wonder we think we find it at all. The criteria we use make it difficult for love to be perceived (hence the difficulty in the search) and militate against its appearance being maintained. It is easier to feel loved by a boyfriend in Connecticut when we are in Toronto or a girlfriend in Vancouver when we live in London. It is not easy to see love on a day-to-day basis.

The irony is this. We look for love in a relationship presumably because someone who loves us will attend to our needs, spend time with us, and give generously—the characteristics of love described above. These are, supposedly, the advantages of being with someone who loves us. He or she is more likely to forgive our weaknesses, treat us kindly, and stay around longer than someone who does not. Defining love by these behaviors would help.

But we seem to have confused the means and ends. Having decided someone loves us, we are willing to accept behavior that would, under other circumstances, be unacceptable. We accept love in lieu of the very behaviors we wanted love to ensure.

The perception of love distorts our perception of events. The decisions we make about how someone feels color our perception of what they are doing. We respond to our theories about their feelings, rather than their actions.

Our theories about how people feel influence our responses as much or even more than our theories about what they are doing. Like other theories, our theories about how people feel are based on our past experiences and our readiness to perceive some things and not others. The same biases which influence our perception of events influence our perception of feelings—in ourselves and in others.

6

Everybody Does It

The similarity with which people see things is remarkable. Though we interpret ambiguity alone, we often agree on what we know and how we feel. The similarities are largely due to culture.

Cultural views of the world reflect widely held assumptions about what is probable, what is meaningful, and how things should and should not be. Television, radio, books, newspapers, and magazines convey these accepted versions of reality. In addition, our schools, religious organizations, families, and therapists transmit cultural assumptions and values.

WHAT WE KNOW

Because we learn about the world from what we read and hear, we internalize our culture's assumptions and values. Like concepts based on direct experience, concepts developed from secondary sources affect our theorizing and influence our behavior. If newspapers, magazines, and television tell us crime in the streets is rampant, we develop concepts about the safety of our city's streets and expectations which influence whether we go out at night, with whom, and at what hours. What we learn influences what we see. We need not have been mugged ourselves, or know someone who has, to assume that the person approaching in the dimly lit parking lot is a drug-crazed mugger, not an insurance salesman.

An intriguing study by George Gerbner illustrates this point.[1] Comparing heavy and light television viewers from the same streets, Gerbner found that people who watch more TV radically overestimate the chance of being mugged and the general danger of city streets compared to less frequent viewers. He concludes that the great incidence of violence and crime portrayed on television—an incidence far in excess of actual street crime—skews probability learning. Viewers learn about their environment, but what they learn is simply not correct. In the face of their erroneous knowledge, they become fearful and passive. According to Gerbner, even those who do not watch TV are affected. The widespread views of those who do pervade our culture. Inaccurate views conveyed by the media are spread by word of mouth.

Because cultural views are widespread and generally accepted, we often fail to question their validity. Later, we lose track of how we know what we know. We forget that our facts may not be accurate and the inferences we draw from them not factual. Of course we make the same mistake with data arising from daily experience. We often forget to check our assumptions and think we understand events that are ambiguous. The point here is that cultural assumptions, those which people around us share, are less likely to be questioned because we assume their accuracy is established.

Cultural myths—traditional, ill-founded, and unexamined views of the world—offer specific explanations to account for what is happening. They offer a basis for judgments about what life is like, for our recognition that something is or is not wrong, and often offer explicit and erroneous remedies for the particular ailment in question. Like any theory, a myth is only one version of reali⁺⁻ ᵀt may fit the data. It may even aid in the solution of particular problems. But the culturally accepted view is only one version of reality, and often it is not functional.

Because "everyone knows" the cultural version of reality, we assume it reflects truth and tend not to generate or test alternative hypotheses when needed, when our constructions do not fit events. Like the primitive witch doctor who knows the incantation must work, we chant louder and faster in the face of failure but do not consider either alternative chants or alternative procedures. If the way to a man's heart is through his stomach, and we have not reached his heart, undoubtedly, we don't cook enough, don't cook well enough, or don't cook like his mother. What else could be the matter?

Consider how myths about marriage and families affect how we see. They influence what we define as proper within families and what we do when things go wrong. The advice, aimed at newlyweds, to "train" their spouses at the start of marriage reflect one such myth. It is based on the untested and untrue assumption that change in behavior is practically impossible. Because change is difficult, the rules and regulations established early in marriage are assumed to be intractable. We must, therefore, make sure mates learn the right rules from the start.

At stake in the train-them-right philosophy are rules about giving and getting: who picks up the underwear, who does the cleaning, who does the cooking, who takes out the garbage, who gets pampered, who gets the breakfast in bed and who gives it. And the reason we are warned at the start is, presumably, because millions of other husbands and wives made the mistake of coddling their spouses early in marriage when they felt like it, and found themselves bringing the breakfast in bed thereafter, long after they stopped feeling like it.

The train-them-right rule entails several additional unspoken assumptions:

(1) Marriage is an adversary relationship. You must negotiate hard at the start or the other guy will get the better of you. When taking an adversary position, gain for one is loss for the other. Dig in and hold the line.

(2) Marital satisfaction need not be mutual. If your husband or wife is miserable, it should not matter to you. You still get breakfast in bed, or the socks picked up. Why change? It's a simplistic model that ignores the fact that a resentful spouse can make life miserable even when bringing the breakfast.

(3) Once a "contract" is established, it need not be renegotiated. You can refuse renegotiation if you have the better deal. You do not have the right or the power to demand renegotiation if you want it. You should have thought about it more at the start. Tough luck. It ignores the fact that the faithful spouse who's been picking up the socks or putting out the garbage for the last ten years can just stop doing it. It denies the freedom we have.

Because the model assumes we have little power to negotiate change, couples caught in train-them-right assumptions find it hard to bargain. The assumption that change is unlikely militates against effort to change. We do not think about how to get the changes we want. The idea of change is itself not very accessible. Specific theories about how to change are not readily available.

The emphasis in our culture on permanence rather than change has the additional effect of blinding us to change when it actually occurs. Like the students described in chapter 3, who do not accurately perceive a playing card of the "wrong" color, we fail to notice changes in the people with whom we deal. Until the gap between our expectations and perceptions becomes so great or so clear as to force our attention, we ignore differences. As much of social interaction is ambiguous, change is easy to ignore.

We believe people are static[2] and imagine we will be with our mates, who will remain essentially the same, for many years. Our assumption that "good" marriages last a long time reflects our underlying assumption that people are unchanging. If people actually changed there would be little reason to think those married at twenty-one would find each other satisfying at fifty.

But people do change and the myth of stability prevents our seeing that change. Two people living together have not one partner but several if they are in tune with what is happening, and several relationships with each other if they negotiate appropriate changes. Unfortunately we don't have a vocabulary for these changes. We rarely admit they exist.

Because we tend not to acknowledge change as real, we do not adjust to it. When our mates say they want to change jobs, or hobbies, or stop going to the cottage, we say they're going through a stage and imply it is a temporary phase from which they will recover. We sometimes say they are going through a stage *again*, suggesting change is frequent, while ignoring its existence.

We ignore change as long as we can, and dismiss it

as a passing aberration when we can no longer ignore it. We are slow to generate theories about what changes mean, and are slow to adjust our relations appropriately. Frequently, *both* spouses in marriage perceive their own development in contrast to their mate's stagnation. It is the cultural tendency to ignore change in others that fosters this perception.

Cultural assumptions about personal change are also reflected in our attitudes toward children and the advice we offer parents about child rearing. Just as we advise newlyweds to train their spouses properly at the first opportunity, we warn new parents not to spoil their children. The underlying assumption is the same.

But what do we mean by "spoiling"? Though we use the term frequently, it is not clear that we know what we mean, or that we all mean the same thing. "Spoiled" usually refers to a child who is demanding, who demands more than we care to give. It does not mean a child who is spoiled (as in vegetables) or ruined, and cannot be reclaimed, though it has that connotation.

But what if his parents are happy giving? Most people say a child is spoiled who demands more than they, the viewers, think the child should get, even if the parents think the behavior satisfactory. It's the case of the onlooker saying, "They are spoiling that child and don't know it." As onlookers we apply our own standards and call children who demand more than we like to give, spoiled.

But more what? The dimension on which people judge children spoiled varies. For some it is money, for some it is time, and for some both are relevant. What counts is determined by the parents', or more properly the viewers', needs—not an objective standard.

Parents who are short on time often think a child who wants a lot of attention is spoiled. Others who have time to spare and enjoy playing with their children do so. The same is true of money. Some parents flinch at a child who asks for a toy each time he wants one; others see nothing wrong with many presents.

But we act as if the child who wants lots of attention now will need constant attention at forty, and the child who wants presents now, will need presents later. We act as if the child is spoiled, or ruined, forever—that habits cannot change. That is the danger. The caution is about the future. "You may be happy now doing all that giving, but watch out," the voice of wisdom tells us, "for times will change." It is actually an admonition to give less than we want at present, of our time or money, against the time we will not want to give.

Like other myths and aphorisms, "Don't spoil them" conveys a variety of messages.

1. It makes assumptions about how children learn, which, at best, considers only part of the process and, at worst, presents a view of children unsupported by current research. It is true that children prefer being carried than left in plastic seats. And it is often more fun to play with someone than to play alone. Children will want what is more fun. But the caution against spoiling suggests they cannot, or will not, learn that sometimes they must play alone, or do without. Some may be slow to learn, but they certainly will learn. They can learn to do without, or do with less, at any point. It only requires that we teach them.

2. The notion of spoiling suggests retraining is almost impossible. The child is spoiled, ruined. So parents are fearful of making new demands (it won't work anyway), and give in quickly to their crying children who will, they think, win in the end. The assumption that it is hard

to change existing behavior patterns becomes a self-fulfilling prophecy.

The data on child rearing does *not* show that children who are deprived find it easier as adults to live with deprivation than children who are not. There is, in fact, some evidence which suggests people who are basically secure handle adversity better than those who are not. They seem to have concepts about controlling their environment which gives them strength to survive difficult times.[3] Those who "know" there is no hope, give up much sooner.

Rules like "Don't spoil them" rest on assumptions which are counter to fact: that children learn by rote and do not interpret, that they are inflexible instead of flexible, that they are incapable of change instead of always changing.

Unfortunately, these assumptions, like all assumptions, affect what we perceive and how we respond to the events we encounter. Cultural myths, by conveying unexamined and untested assumptions, influence what we "know" about the world, though what we know might not be so.

What to Want

Culture does more than teach us about our environment. It tells us not only how things are, but how things should be, what we should want, what we should be, and how we should behave. Even when we do not want it, we know what our culture values. To the extent that we know the rules, even if we do not accept them, culture influences how we evaluate what we perceive, what we strive for, and what we demand of ourselves and others.

In our culture the consensus about what is desirable is strong. We are more likely to differ over means than ends. We generally want what we are supposed to: friends, families, nice homes, and good jobs. On the whole we agree how these assets should be defined.

There are, of course, many allowable differences within our culture regarding what we are supposed to want. Because we live in a society which is somewhat tolerant of diversity, diversity exists. What is defined as desirable often varies between ethnic groups, religious groups, classes, and sexes. We usually want what we are supposed to want as a member of these groups.

When we do not want what we know we are supposed to want tension arises. The discrepancy between what we know our culture values and what we want will attract our attention; we will try to resolve the discrepancy.

We might revise our theories about what is desirable. This option results in conformity. Alternatively, we might consider our culture's assumptions and decide *they* are inappropriate. Thirdly, we might redefine the relationship between what our culture values and what we want in such a way that the two become compatible.

Conformity. Consider conformity first. The pressure to conform, what we usually call social pressure, arises from several sources. Peter, for example, may be content with his salary; he earns enough for his family, likes his current position, and likes not working hard. His wife, Maria, may share his values. But both may think he should get a promotion. They think so because our culture generally assumes people should move up. Professional advancement is considered good. The "goodness" is not questioned. Given that everyone knows it is good to get promoted, and the fact we are constantly reminded of it, it's not surprising that Peter and Maria notice his "failure" to get promoted after many years at the job. There is pressure to conform to the ideal simply to resolve discrepancy.

A second pressure comes from external sources. Peter and his wife are not the only ones who have noticed the gap between the fantasy of frequent promotions and the facts. Their parents may ask why Peter hasn't been promoted. Such questions seem to support the cultural view that promotion is good and make it unlikely the couple will resolve their conflict by concluding that promotions are irrelevant. If "everyone else" thinks promotions are valuable, maybe they are. Of course, parents and friends think promotions valuable because they also have accepted the cultural view uncritically.

A third pressure, which is perceived as external, is in fact internal. It is the pressure Peter and Maria generate by assuming people who have not commented on Peter's lack of promotion are wondering about it. This assumption is not irrational. Discrepancy from expectation catches attention. That is why Peter, Maria, their parents, and their friends have noticed he has not been promoted. They imagine others have also noticed. They are probably correct.

Unfortunately, our culture tells us not only what people should strive for, but how to interpret their failure to behave in the expected fashion. In Peter's case the ready explanation to account for a failure at promotion—especially if the man hired after him got the promotion he did not get—is failure. But Peter did not fail. He did not get promoted because he did not try. He did not work hard because he likes his leisure time and likes his present job. He is not ambitious. Ironically, because that is not a ready or even credible interpretation in our culture the chances that Peter will be believed are slim. He knows this. He might not believe someone else in a similar situation. He may like his leisure but not like to be considered incompetent. Next time he may work to get promoted.

What is interesting about the "what they think" dilemma is that the pressure it exerts on people is real. It is a real pressure, from a culture that conveys assumptions about how we should live. And while it is true, as psychologists tell us, that we would not be susceptible to the pressure if it were not in our own heads, it is not only in our own heads (a fact they tend to overlook). We have been living and learning in this culture and are not immune to its demands.

We have been too cavalier about the messages that get communicated covertly in our society about what things mean. We underestimate the effects of myths upon our lives. We think that simply becoming aware of the myth frees us from its influence. Unfortunately, it is not that simple. To begin, it is not so easy to unlearn what we've learned when culture continues supporting the early view. But myths have a power over and above anxiety and guilt. They influence theory making. Even if Peter doesn't care about getting promoted, others will make meaning from his behavior. The myths will affect the meaning they make, will influence their behavior toward him, and subsequently his theory making.

There have been many studies in the last ten years on the effect of full-time working mothers on families and children. There have been no studies of the effect of full-time working fathers on their families (we study unemployed fathers instead). It is clear how we think about working mothers.[4] Though over one third of North American women work full-time, it is obvious our culture assumes it is better if they didn't. The converse is true of men. It is quite remarkable that the studies show no ill effects. Working women know they are violating what society still assumes is the best course of action. This might make them anxious (what if they are making a mistake), might make their husbands apprehensive ("Would she still be working if I earned more money?"), and might make their children resentful if they think she "shouldn't" be working. Some actions seem to require justification.

Imagine Margo forgetting her husband Andras' birthday. Even if he doesn't care about birthdays, the event takes on significance because they both know a wife is supposed to remember her husband's birthday. She may begin to wonder why she forgot. What does it mean about her feelings for him? She thinks she loves him, but why would she forget his birthday? He may also wonder why she forgot. He knows the omission is not significant and must push the thought from his mind. When the fifth person asks him what Margo bought him and he explains for the fifth time that she forgot his birthday, the feeling that maybe something is wrong, though he knows it isn't, has become an irritation. He must excuse her behavior.

They are both aware that her failure to get a present reflects on their marriage. And it does. It may show they are comfortable enough not to worry over token displays of affection. But they know that others will construct, perhaps unconsciously, a theory about this particular omission which probably will not jive with theirs. If we are raised to believe that presents reflect feelings it is hard to develop alternative explanations that justify her omission.

Rejection of Cultural Values. Discrepancies between what our culture values and what we value can also be resolved by reevaluating the cultural assumptions we have internalized. Margo and Andras might, for example, decide that presents reflect a petty middle-class concern with visible consumption, not a symbolic display of affection, and decide as a matter of principle not to exchange presents. In doing this they reinterpret what it means to give gifts in our society and alleviate a great deal of the pressure described above. It is, after all, not the gift that counts but what giving or not giving means. If they change the meaning there is no cause for worry. A discrepancy no longer exists. Gifts are seen as negative and they do not give them.

The same technique works to diffuse the social pressure they feel when others ask what Margo gave him. By explaining that the omission was deliberate, and supplying a means by which the omission can be interpreted, they offer an explanation that was not previously accessible. They decrease the probability of others or themselves making negative interpretations.

Making Ideas Compatible. The third option is to accept both the cultural definition of what is desirable and our own definition of what is desirable, and define the relationship between these in such a way that they become compatible.

Prior to the 1960s when the women's movement began, many occupations were, and still are, defined as unfeminine—not suitable for women. Few women wanted to enter "masculine" professions in the 1960s because they accepted the cultural definition of femininity. The feminist revolution, a revolution in thinking, came when women who wanted lives previously defined as inappropriate, or masculine, argued they be allowed to live them without stigma.

As always happens when people behave in ways that are discrepant from expectation, onlookers—both male and female—attempted to interpret the feminists' behavior. (No one interpreted the behavior of women who went into nursing, that was expected. Instead, we interpreted the behavior of women who wanted promotion to executive positions, who wanted acceptance to medical school, and women who wanted to work in construction.) An accessible interpretation during the 1960s was that these women were masculine, perhaps even homosexual. Why, the media asked, would normal heterosexual, feminine women want to do such obviously masculine work? And it seems that the women's movement made little progress and had only narrow appeal so long as it argued that these jobs were not masculine and that feminists were "normal" women. The cultural pressure to perceive certain jobs as masculine was great; a few dedicated women could not alter those definitions.

Momentum came to the movement when the argument switched. Women's liberation gained wide support from women and men across the country when it stopped trying to redefine existing cultural categories and appealed to an already existing and highly valued cultural ideal which was compatible with their aims. At some point we stopped talking about whether women who drive trucks are masculine and started talking about individual freedom, equal rights, discrimination, and equal pay for equal work. The previously incongruous demands were given new meaning related to existing and accepted cultural values. The behavior of radical women was redefined. It no longer reflected their sexual attitudes, or their rebellious nature, but their willingness to fight for individual freedom. North Americans favor individual freedom, or are afraid to say they do not.

WHAT TO SEE

In addition to teaching about the world and what is valuable, culture suggests what is important in particular situations, and what portions of events warrant attention.

It directs attention. In this sense culture acts to minimize our perception of some events and sharpen our perception of others by defining some but not others as significant. By influencing what we attend to culture affects what we see and which of the myriad potential discrepancies we are likely to encounter.

We are most familiar with the direction of attention in movies. When introducing a scene, a dinner party for example, the camera usually presents what moviemakers call an establishing shot. This is a broad view of the room and is called "establishing" because it establishes the context. The context is also established by preceding scenes so that this is not a dinner party in isolation but perhaps a dinner party following a family fight. Context is always embedded in still larger contexts, like frames within frames.

Having established context we attend more closely to important aspects of the scene. In real life, as in movies, context usually defines what is important. If we are watching a film about marital discord, the camera might zoom closely on the husband in question as he glances across the table and sees his wife flirting. The camera "looks at" what is important in particular contexts. We do the same in daily life. It is unlikely, given the context described above, that we would in our culture get a close-up of the silverware.

The impact of attention lies exactly in this narrowing of perception. If we watch the husband or wife in this scene, we do not see what else is happening—to others in the room, for example. Because we focus narrowly, on the assumption we are attending to the only area of importance, we do not learn about events outside our observations. We encounter discrepancies only within our area of regard and respond to the area of observation, not events outside it. In this way culture tells us where to look and what to see.

WHAT TO FEEL

Culture also affects the way we feel. Consider John and Alia Fleming, who are giving the dinner party described above. We can see the impact of culture both on the fight they have before their guests arrive and on their feelings at the party later that night.

The fight itself, typical of many family squabbles, reflects a strong cultural influence. Alia, a well-socialized female, "knows" that her family and children are more important than her work; that relationships take priority in her life; that the maintenance of relationships and the nurturance of her children require an expenditure of time and effort which is amply rewarded. She works full-time at a job which is superficially the same as John's (they are both illustrators for a major commercial artist) but considers her work of secondary importance. Though she values her career, she cannot imagine pulling more time from her children to further her professional status. The children need someone to work with at night on spelling and arithmetic; they need someone to confide in when they are frightened; they need someone to pick them up at 6 P.M. when they are tired after swimming. The evening hours between five and nine are, to her, crucial.

John also says his family comes first but the words mean something different to him. He knows his career is more important than spelling, arithmetic, and a prolonged discussion of the latest school play. If the kids want to take swimming, he argues, they can damn well take the subway home. If he does not make department head next year, there may not be another opportunity.

Who will pay for all those lessons? Besides, he couldn't stand to stay at his old job with Ed, who is younger than he, working as his boss. He "needs" that promotion. If Alia thinks the kids need coddling, she can do it herself.

The discrepancy in their views is largely determined by culture. They fight about John's working hours. Alia says he should get home earlier (especially the night of their party!); he says he "cannot."

Culture also influences how Alia interprets John's lateness. Our culture offers several ready interpretations for such lateness and, in effect, offers the list of theories from which Alia selects (based on personal experience) the most "likely" options. She "knows" he's been working. In some cultures John's religious habits might come into question. Presumably, Alia would feel differently if she thought John was communing with spirits or having an affair from five to nine each evening.

Thirdly, culture influences how Alia and John feel because it influences the way they label emotion in different contexts. In situations culturally defined as hostile (a fight) the probability of labeling arousal "anger" is great; in situations defined as "cheerful" (a party) the probability of labeling arousal positively is greater. Interestingly, Alia and John sometimes bring different contexts (frames) to the same situation. When John came home before their party, he entered a situation he defined as happy; he was going to a party and labeled his arousal "excitement." It took him a while to understand why Alia was fighting. In her mind, the situation was defined and framed by a different set of events: his habitual lateness. Given the way she framed the situation and labeled her arousal (anger), their argument seemed appropriate.[5]

Culture even tells the Flemings how they are supposed to feel in certain circumstances;[6] sad at funerals, joyous at weddings. When they don't feel "properly" they notice that something is wrong. The difference between what they know they should feel, and what they do feel, creates tension and arousal; sometimes they label that feeling "guilt": I should feel loving toward my child, but I feel angry; I should feel happy but I'm depressed; I should feel sad (that my rich cousin died), but I feel happy. Culture tells them to feel guilty about feeling inappropriately, and what they should have felt in the first place.

But John and Alia blame each other for their failure to feel happy. They know they should feel happy (it's a party) and think they would have if the other wouldn't have "ruined the evening" (by getting home late; by picking a fight). Because they blame *each other* for their failure to feel "partyish" they label their arousal "anger." Earlier, they were angry about the lateness/fight. Now they are angry because they are not happy.

By influencing the way they label emotion, culture also tells the Flemings how to respond. If angry they fight, if sad they cry, if happy they laugh. Because the teaching of culture is pervasive and powerful, they usually see, feel, and act appropriately.

SIMILARITIES AND DIFFERENCES IN PERCEPTION

The above episode also shows that an important source of disagreement in perception comes from culture. Our culture is not unidimensional, and, as was mentioned earlier, conveys somewhat different messages to people of different social classes and different sexes.

We all know that men and women are treated differently within our culture. The experience of being male is different from the experience of being female (just as the experience of being middle class is different from the experience of being working class). Men and women are taught to value different commodities and events, to expect different behavior from others and to learn which behaviors appropriate to one sex are inappropriate to the other. As a result, men and women develop concepts which differ as a function of their sex and class. (It is no accident that Alia and John fight over many of the same things that thousands of other middle-class heterosexual couples fight about.) Culture tells its men and women what to see and how to feel about what they see.

We should therefore expect to find systematic differences in the way different sexes, classes, and age groups in our culture perceive events. They interpret on the basis of their past experiences, which are regularly affected by sex, class, and age. They then attend to events which present discrepancies from their different expectations. Interestingly, systematic differences in attention perpetuate differences in what they see and what they learn, even in situations that seem, superficially, the same.

part

II

AMBIGUITY
AND
INTERACTION

7

Seeing Differently

People who live together or spend a great deal of time together often make meaning from the "same" events. But they cannot share one view of events, or share one another's perceptions. They make meaning individually and, as a result, must live with ambiguity. What is really intended, what has actually occurred, must always be inferred.

There are, of course, many times that couples construe things similarly. The Levins' perception of Norman's illness is a case in point. They had been married for five years when Norm's parents, who lived far from the couple, announced they were finally coming for a visit. Both Sheila and Norm appeared happy. Two days before his parents were to arrive, Norm, who had not been sick once since Sheila knew him, took ill. His parents had to postpone the visit. In this instance both Sheila and Norm, psychologically "sophisticated" people, concluded on the basis of Norm's general health, and the fact that they were both a bit nervous before the visit, that Norm got sick because he did not want his parents to visit. In looking to explain the illness, they agreed about what happened.

But that does not make them right. It is just as possible that Norm would have gotten sick that day had his parents not been coming. His co-worker had the flu the previous week and it isn't obvious that psychological factors were at work. Nonetheless, Sheila and Norm were comfortable in their understanding and shared the same perception, or construction, of reality.

Imagine how different the situation might have been if it were Sheila's parents who were coming to visit, and Norm, who does not like her parents, got sick. In this case Norm might deny that psychological factors had any part in his illness and would, with some alacrity, point out that his co-worker had had the flu. If Sheila continued to assume the illness was psychologically motivated, Norm would feel misunderstood and unfairly criticized; especially as he feels sick and wants sympathy. Sheila might feel angry and resentful. Her parents come only once in five years and Norman gets sick.

Couples experience similar realities if they make comparable interpretations of ambiguous events. To the extent they share similar concepts and generate compatible theories all seems to go well. Problems sometimes arise when people interpret events dissimilarly.

DIFFERENCES IN PERCEPTION

Because each person in a family constructs his or her own reality, family life and friendships are often a far cry from what many of us expect. Instead of going through life side by side with a person or persons who will share our lives, we are surrounded by people who will always see things somewhat differently. The deeper we probe, the more likely we are to see the differences.

Many couples have had the following experience discussing a restaurant they have been to or a vacation they have shared. You begin by saying it was good, or bad. A point you agree on. And though you each think you know why you agree, you find when questioned that you do not. While you liked the scenery, your mate liked the hotel, which you found satisfactory but nothing special. Your mate, it turns out, loved the wide open beaches, which you also enjoyed, though you prefer a pool to the ocean. You both liked the vacation and your mate would like to go back, but you would not.

The same thing happens regarding people. You both agree you like the couple who has just moved down the street. Upon further discussion it turns out one of you likes the wife and can tolerate the husband, while the other likes the husband and can tolerate the wife. To you her strong point is her sense of humor; your spouse thinks she has neither personality nor a sense of humor. To your spouse the husband is exciting; to you, frenetic.

Differences in perception also occur regarding ourselves and our families. For some, these differences are disconcerting, for others exciting. The fact remains that we cannot know the same reality, though the realities we construct and the interpretations we make may be similar.

The issue is further complicated because we cannot say with certainty which view of the neighbors, the in-laws, or the children is "correct." People are complex and operate from a confusion of many motives. A single perspective on anyone's behavior, while attractive to the viewer, is at best a favorite theory and not an explanation. A variety of theories will fit any behavior.

When we say we know people well, we usually mean that they behave in a fashion congruent with our theory about how they will behave. Their behavior may fit our theory; that does not make our theory "right."

Susan, for example, knew her husband liked to eat as soon as he came home from work. Her father had liked to eat as soon as he came home and she always went out of her way to have dinner ready for her husband promptly at six, just as her mother had for her father. Bob never told Sue he did not like eating early as he thought eating early was important *to her*. Because she was so obviously fanatic about having dinner promptly, his assumption that she wanted to eat at six did not seem presumptive. It seemed self-evident. As Bob never said he didn't like eating right after he got home, that he'd rather read the paper or listen to the news, Sue had no reason to doubt her assumptions about his preferences. He always arrived on time and ate heartily. The question of time never entered her mind. She knew that "men like to eat when they get home," and therefore thought she knew what Bob liked. For both Sue and Bob, the behavior of the other was predictable, and fit their theories. The behavior fit, but the theories were wrong.

Because events are ambiguous, we see and hear what we expect. Even if it's negative, we hear what we expect. Several years ago a colleague asked a friend of mine about an article she had published. The subject no longer interested her and she was, in fact, feeling a bit embarrassed about the article. With the clarity of hindsight, the article appeared to her both trivial and poorly executed. At the end of the conversation, which she did her best to keep brief, he looked her straight in the eyes and enunciated in his best British accent, laden with sarcasm, that "the article sounds most interesting." To which she replied, equally sarcastically, "I'm delighted you think so," and left.

Sanity hit at the other side of the door and she didn't

go far. She was actually so shocked that this otherwise proper and polite individual would attack her directly (she could imagine a more subtle maneuver), she stopped to review the conversation and make sure she had heard correctly. Of course she had heard the words. It's the intonation that was open to doubt and in this case the meaning depended on intonation. It also struck her that her Philadelphia-trained ear might not know British sarcasm if she heard it and might hear it when none was intended. In any event, she went back to his office and explained that his "most interesting" had sounded sarcastic. At that point he assured her it had not been. He was interested in the article, even if she wasn't, and could not understand why she had so blatantly attacked *him* as soon as he complimented her work.

A similar incident occurred a few years earlier when I took a typing job one summer during college, after lying about how fast I typed. At the end of the day, the professor for whom I was typing came out to say how pleased he was with my work. I was actually such a poor typist I hadn't taken lunch that day in an effort to turn in a reasonable amount of work and hold the job at least two days before anyone caught on. I can remember clearly the long silence after his praise as I debated whether to simply say "thank you" or assure him I'd work harder tomorrow. As most of us judge ourselves more harshly than others, this tendency to hear criticism when none exists is widespread.

The tendency to see what we expect operates even more powerfully in families. But because we think we know each other well we are less likely than in work situations to notice ambiguities. If you "know" for example that your wife does not like your new suit, her "That looks nice on you, dear" sounds insulting. If your husband almost always complains about your lack of culinary expertise, his remark to friends that his wife "is some cook" sounds like an attack. When you feel inadequate as a parent and guilty about not doing better, a child's remark that he wishes he lived with your neighbor, who knows how to treat kids properly, cuts to the quick. We think we know what was intended, assume that only one meaning fits, and fail to consider alternative interpretations.

We also hear positive remarks when none is intended. If you've just cooked an original chicken recipe, which to you tastes superb, the question "Where did you get this recipe?" is heard as a compliment instead of a neutral question or a statement of disbelief. If you are eager for a night at the movies, the question "Did you get a baby-sitter?" is heard as a request to go out when in fact your mate may hope you can spend the evening home. And if you are wearing the dress you "know" your husband admires, his question about whether it "always had that (gasp) white trimming" will prove his appreciation of its styling. If you're in the proper mood, your child's remark that you're terrible parents might even be taken as sarcasm—a good joke from an appreciative child—and rewarded with a hug. It depends on your own mental set and context.

COMPATIBLE PERCEPTIONS

But life is more than mental set and context. The people we live with are real people, with real needs, real feelings, real emotions, and a tendency to behave in particular fashions. We do not imagine that our spouses or children sometimes slam doors loudly while stomping to the kitchen. The slamming and stomping are real. As are the laughter and joking on other occasions. What varies is our perception of the meaning behind their actions, and their perception of the meaning behind our actions.

The extent to which our perceptions agree or disagree, and the specific areas of agreement or disagreement, determine in large measure the kind and quality of life we share.

Relationships which are "bad," in contrast to those which are "good," differ largely in the extent to which the people involved are comfortable with each other's reality. That is why it is hard to tell by simply looking whether a particular marriage works. It is why we're often surprised that the happy couple down the street decided to divorce, or that the couple who throw dishes at each other are still together. We can't guess how they feel because it's the meaning they give to each other's behavior, not the behavior itself, that is important.

It's not what one has in a relationship or even how one is treated that counts. It's how we interpret what is happening that is crucial. The most acceptable behavior from the outside may be perceived as unacceptable by those involved.

Carla feels smothered by her husband, Josef. He calls her at the office twice a day, questions her in detail when she gets home, and asks repeatedly about where she is going and what she plans to do. She finds him overly attentive, overly protective, and overly curious about every detail of her life. Carla envies her friend Vivian, whose marriage seems less restrictive.

Vivian and Pierre spend a great deal of time apart and, it seems to Carla, do not keep track of each other's business. But to Vivian the relationship is not so rosy. According to her, Pierre does not care what happens to her, has too many outside interests, and hardly notices her existence. He never calls her at the office, never asks about her day, and doesn't care who she sees when he is not around.

Each woman finds her husband's behavior upsetting; one because she thinks he doesn't trust her, the other because she thinks he does not care about her. They are not happily married. They do not have "good husbands."

But there is no such thing as a good wife or good husband in the abstract. Vivian might be happy with Josef, her friend's husband, if she perceived his attention as affection, not distrust. And Carla might be happy with Pierre if she interpreted his detachment as trust, not disregard. Each woman would be happier with her own husband if she interpreted his behavior differently.

Similarly, the "goodness" of parents, children, and friends cannot be evaluated separate from their interactions. The Weisses, who need lots of sleep, read for hours each day, and consider a walk to the grocer a week's worth of physical activity, define their energetic daughter as troublesome. She always bothers them to go to the park, pesters them to play ball, plays loudly and boisterously with friends, and generally disturbs her parents' quiet routine. They are more likely to define her as a problem than they would a child whose energy level is more attuned to theirs. They might be happier with Tony, the quiet boy next door. His athletic and high energy parents consider him a problem because he never wants to go on hikes, hates touch football, and would, if they let him, spend all his free time reading.

The children's perception of whether they have "good" parents is influenced by the same considerations. The daughter in the first instance probably finds her parents somewhat rejecting. They hardly want to play, refuse to do what she likes doing, and generally lack a sense of fun or adventure. Tony might also find his parents selfish. They don't encourage his reading, nag him constantly about what he should be doing, and drag him as often as possible on long and boring field trips.

CHANGES IN PERCEPTION

The issue of "good" versus "bad" relationships is further complicated because we often *change* the meaning we give to behavior. We can go for weeks without being upset by our children's messy room and suddenly feel angered and upset when we notice the disarray on Monday morning. By the same token, the disorder that usually annoys us as we trip from the closet to the chest of drawers seems perfectly innocuous at other times. The skateboard that often looms as a major hazard, on other days gets kicked to the corner without presenting a problem. The meaning we give to the mess and to our offspring's failure to tidy their rooms changes.

My friend Judy usually assumes her husband, Jeremy, is too busy or simply too disinterested in housekeeping to be much help. He shares the same view of himself. So she does not expect Jeremy to do much work around the house (he does other chores) and is pleasantly surprised if he feels moved to wash a few dishes. But now and again her perception of his behavior, or in this case his *lack* of relevant behavior, changes. She goes through periods, particularly when she is tired or overworked, when his tendency to ignore household tasks looks suddenly more like manipulation than oversight. At such times she "knows" darn well that he counts on her doing the work and takes advantage of the fact that she will do it.

When in this alternate reality my friend is angry not only because her husband does not help, but also because his action seems deliberate and offensive. Jeremy, on the other hand, feels attacked and maligned by her accusations. Why, he wonders, does his wife suddenly turn on him for not helping when he hardly ever helps and she hardly ever seems to mind? What are her real motives? Is she manipulating him? They now disagree, and will fight about what is happening.

To me, what is interesting is not whether Jeremy cleans the house, why Jeremy does or does not help, or even why Judy sometimes cares and sometimes doesn't. What intrigues me is that whether Judy and Jeremy define themselves as happy in any given week hinges primarily on the assumption they make about each other's behavior. It's the *changes in meaning* that count, not the behavior *per se*.

Changes in meaning sometimes occur over longer time periods. When Mary first met her husband, a college professor, she admired him greatly for his erudite mind and found his tendency to be absentminded charming and lovable. He couldn't, she smiled, get through the day without her. As a result, as soon as they married she started attending to his every need. She laid out his clothes in the morning, reminded him of all his appointments, planned all their social activities, and gave him directions whenever he drove because she knew, although he'd driven the route many times before, he wouldn't remember. (She wouldn't do the driving herself, she said, because a man likes to feel like the boss.) At the start of their marriage the arrangement worked beautifully. Mary was happy to have someone to take care of, and had found a satisfying way to express her devotion. James, who had a full and trying career, was happy to be cared for and delighted to be freed from the nitty-gritty of daily life. It seemed to work well.

It's not clear when the change first started. When I met Mary after her seventh year of marriage, she was upset and angry. Her husband could do nothing right. He could hardly dress himself in the morning, forgot appointments if she didn't remind him, and couldn't find his way to her sister's house though they'd been there a hundred times.

James was also angry. His wife, it seems, was putting him down. She had no confidence in his ability. He felt he was losing control. She was always so sure he'd make mistakes, he got nervous about trying, and did just what he was trying to avoid. He didn't even know the way to his sister-in-law's. How could he learn if every time he got to an intersection his wife would tell him where to turn? He never needed to remember. How could he develop confidence?

By the time I met her, Mary was afraid to let James do anything by himself. She was sure he would make a mistake. And James was no longer certain, after years of enforced helplessness, that he would not. Ironically, the behavior that each had found especially attractive years before had changed its meaning. To James his wife was no longer nurturant but destructive. And Mary had, for quite a while, found James incompetent, not absent-minded. Once they started making negative interpretations of each other's behavior, the behavior they saw fit their theories.

All relationships change over time. Individuals change and circumstances change. Often, like Mary and James, we simply define people's actions so they look quite different. Behavior itself is not crucial. The way we interpret behavior and whether our interpretations mesh in a compatible and satisfying fashion are more important.

8

Doing It Together

We are often unaware of how differently we interpret behavior. Mary and James, described in the previous chapter, have entirely different views of themselves and their relationship. She sees herself as efficient; he thinks she is overbearing. She sees him as incompetent; he sees himself as overburdened. We know they perceive themselves differently. But they are not aware of their differences. She assumes he knows he is incompetent and does not understand why he resents her help. He assumes she knows she is overbearing and does not understand why she does not change.

They are unaware that their interpretations do not mesh. As a result, they are unaware of the ambiguity in many of their conversations. Often they think they are agreeing when they are not—this leads to future disagreement. At other times they think they understand why they are fighting though they do not. They do not check on whether they understand each other correctly, or take care to convey ideas clearly. They assume they perceive each other clearly and congruently—though they do not like what they see. Their failure to note the differences in what they see affects their interaction.

They cannot, of course, eliminate ambiguity. No matter how clearly they speak, how unambiguously they know their minds, or how directly they deal with each other, they must make meaning from what is said. They will often misconstrue each other's meaning—even when they check. But they can decrease the probability of being misunderstood and of misunderstanding.

As speakers they could take care to say what they mean and check that the other understands what they wish to convey. As listeners, they could check that they have understood correctly, and ask for clarification when they need it.

Because communication is always ambiguous, we are forever wondering what things mean. During dinner negotiations, when a friend says, "I don't think you'll like that restaurant," does he really think you won't like that restaurant, think it's too expensive, feel like eating something else, or prefer grabbing a bite at home and going to a film instead? When a ten-year-old child says he hates school and isn't learning anything, is it true that he is bored at school, or is the work too hard? When a friend turns down your invitation to dinner for the third straight time, is she really very busy? Does she no longer like you, does she like you but not your other guests, does she hate dinner parties, or is she depressed? When the personnel manager says, "I would hire you but I'm not sure we have the money," does he really like you? Is he really short on money, or think you are unqualified?

Our previous experience with individuals largely determines how we interpret their present behavior, but it cannot be taken as proof we are interpreting correctly. A wife who thinks her husband is usually manipulative is likely to interpret his behavior as manipulative—though she may be wrong about both his past and present actions. In the same way, a wife who thinks her husband is selfless and honest is likely to interpret his behavior as selfless, whether or not it is.

The way we interpret remarks determines how we respond and how we feel about the interaction. A woman who trusts her mate's judgment regarding taste in restaurants responds one way to his suggestions. If she believes her mate is stingy and manipulative she responds another way. The mother who believes her son consistently gets in trouble responds one way to his stories about school; the mother who trusts her son acts differently.

SOURCES OF ERROR

There are a variety of reasons we do not ask people to clarify what they mean. One reason is fear. And that fear is generated by a variety of different motives. We are afraid, for instance, of hearing something we do not want to hear. We would rather not know immediately that we did not get the job we want. We do not want to be told directly. It is sometimes better not to know.

There is also the fear of appearing stupid for not knowing what someone means. We think we should understand the people we are talking with even when they speak obscurely. We often assume that any problem in communication is our own. The fear of looking stupid in the face of vagueness nicely illustrates our culture's denial of ambiguity. Remarks made to us are not ambiguous; we just don't understand them sometimes.

The problem is compounded by our embarrassment about what we hope a person has said, which inhibits us from asking. People in dating situations often are aware and take advantage of this reluctance to ask for clarification. Both men and women know how effective certain ambiguous remarks about the future can be with a person who hopes to see you again. Obviously the stereotypic sweet young woman in Hollywood movies cannot look at her male counterpart and ask, "Does that mean you would like *me* to share the little cottage, or simply that you'd like to have one?" She is supposed to know.

In fact, by perceiving ambiguity and asking for clarification the young lady above risks looking stupid (for not knowing the answer or not knowing she was not supposed to ask) or desperate, as she needed to know the answer so badly she was willing to break the taboo against asking. Words are often inappropriate.

Unfortunately, the taboo against recognizing mystification (or asking for clarity) prevents appropriate action. If the young woman assumes her hero is proposing, she may be rudely surprised at a later date. Alternatively, she might assume he is only discussing his preference for shingled-over stucco cottages—and ignore what he considers a clear proposal. She would be better off if she recognized that their conversation is ambiguous. Knowing that she does not know what he means opens the possibility of learning.

Once she makes an interpretation, it is difficult for her to discover an error. Having heard a proposal of marriage, she would need considerable data which contradicts that perception before she would revise her thinking. In fact, it is unlikely she would ever conclude she was wrong about the proposal and might, upon seeing her fiancé in the arms of another woman, assume he was unfaithful or had changed his mind, not that she had heard him wrong.

Many disagreements arise because ambiguous communication has allowed two or more people to follow the same conversation while making different interpretations of what they hear. At a later time, when confronted with the failure to fulfill each other's expectations, bad intentions, not errors of interpretation, are blamed.

The point is not just that interaction is ambiguous. We know that. But we do not live as if we know it. We forget that we and the people with whom we interact are meaning makers, that we construe events.

In scientific studies of perception and communication distortions due to interpretation can be clearly shown. Unfortunately, the demands of daily living preclude the sterile clarity of laboratory research. In real life, we are often unaware of the ambiguity in our behavior. Because the responses we get are also ambiguous, we often fail to notice misunderstandings when they occur. We operate under imperfect conditions which increase the chance of error, and decrease the chance of error being discovered.

FAILURE TO SAY ENOUGH

The following presents a brief dialogue between Marty and his wife, Fiona, who are planning a weekend vacation. The relation between the words spoken, the intended meaning, the listener's response, and the listener's intention are shown.

Fiona (Spoken):	Let's go away for a weekend soon.
Fiona (Intended):	Let's go away next weekend. I'm getting desperate for a break.
Marty (Spoken):	That sounds good.
Marty (Intended):	I'll think about it later.
Fiona S:	I think I'd like to go to Mendocino since we haven't been there yet.
Fiona I:	I want to go to Mendocino.

Marty S: Tahoe's supposed to be nice.

Marty I: I don't feel like making a decision now. Let's think about different places.

Fiona S: Mendocino is closer.

Fiona I: I don't want to go to Tahoe. I don't think you want to go to Mendocino.

Marty S: Maybe the Smiths would like to go someplace with us.

Fiona S: Maybe.

Fiona I: Why the hell are you bringing up the Smiths? We'll never be able to organize something with the Smiths by next week. You're stalling.

Marty S: What's on television?

Marty I: I'd rather watch TV than make plans; I'm tired.

Fiona S: There's a movie on.

Fiona I: You dummy. You never want to take a vacation and always change the subject on me.

In this example Fiona hesitates to ask directly for what she wants—to go away next weekend. She may be afraid of her husband, afraid he will laugh at her suggestion or tell her she does not, or should not, need a rest. Because she does not ask directly, he may not know what she wants. By not being direct she increases the probability of being disappointed. Later, because she is sure she knows, she does not ask why he has changed the subject. As a result, she remains locked in her preconceived and erroneous construction of reality, a construction that militates against her getting what she wants.

Marty in turn may be acting from lethargy, though he seems unkind to her. Fiona has been overworked and is overtired. He is aware of her problem but is too tired himself to make plans for a vacation and thinks it better to consider alternatives and plan for further ahead. He does not tell her he does not want to discuss the subject because he thinks she will be hurt by his refusal. He thinks he has handled the situation well by allowing a short discussion and showing he is interested before settling down to the game. He may have no idea she is angry and resentful. She knows she is angry but assumes he knows and doesn't tell him.

FAILURE TO SAY IT CLEARLY

Hesch S: Marge, could you pick up a roll of film for me today? I have six appointments, am unprepared for my meeting, and have to get my laundry at the other end of town. Goddammit, where are my shoes?

Hesch I: Marge, please help me. I have more to do today than I can possibly get done. I'm afraid I won't get through the day successfully. I'm shooting outdoor scenes for the magazine tomorrow morning and won't be home until late tonight.

Marge S: I'm pretty busy, but I'll do it if I get a chance.

Marge I: What are you complaining for? If you'd stop leaving things for the last minute you wouldn't get into spots like that. I have enough to do myself with shopping, the kids, and the house cleaning for tomorrow night's company. I'll get it if I pass a store. How should *I* know where you left your shoes?

Hesch S: Thanks.

Hesch I: Thank God you'll get it.

That night:

Hesch S: Where is the film you got me?

Marge S: I didn't get a chance.

Hesch S: Goddammit, I told you I needed that film.

Hesch I: You're impossible. You don't do anything but take care of the house and kids and I ask you for a little help and you don't care enough to do it.

Marge S: You did not tell me you *needed* the film. I had a busy day.

Marge I: You louse. What gives you the right to come home and treat me like that? Get your own film.

Marge and Hesch both failed to check each other's meaning. In the morning he did not make a clear request for the film he needed. As a result, Marge couldn't judge how much effort to expend on getting it and did not know why she felt "leaned on" by her husband, who was obviously in a bad mood when he left the house. She even felt blamed because he couldn't find his shoes, though his remark was probably rhetorical.

By evening when Hesch comes home looking for support and nurturance Marge is tired and would also like some comfort. Unfortunately, neither makes the request. Instead she gets blamed for not fulfilling the request Hesch *intended* to make but did not. He interprets her failure as more than a failure to get film. It's a failure to respond to his needs, to show that she cares about him. On the other side, she believes that if he really cared he would understand she was busy all day and needed some rest herself. Each feels put down and rejected, unloved.

Because they feel they cannot rely on each other, and are afraid the other does not care about them, they will be careful in the future not to reveal their vulnerability. So the need for support and nurturance will remain unspoken. Both will be afraid to say, "I need your help," while resenting that they do not get enough. If they do not state their requests more clearly, and check their interpretations of each other's statements the probability of misunderstanding will remain high. Each will be locked in his own negative interpretation of the other's behavior.

In this case, a direct request from Hesch or a simple question by Marge such as "Do you need the film today or can it wait if I'm busy?" would have interrupted the cycle. He might have also saved the day by noting she did not promise to get the film unless she got a chance. His assumption that she would get the chance, based on his perception of what her day was like, was obviously erroneous. They might both have ended the day more happily if either had risked saying they feel rejected and unloved so the issue might be clarified. As both assume they *are* unloved there appears no reason to discuss the issue.

FAILURE TO SAY ANYTHING

In some cases, the interpretations we make are based on the other person's actions and expressions more than on words. In making meaning it makes little difference which information is used; it is the interpretation that counts. A friend of mine took a trip with her husband one Saturday which illustrates the point perfectly. The two of them and their two young children set out for a pleasant drive in the country which quickly turned into one of those confusing family afternoons we all hope to avoid. Her kids started squabbling, the traffic was heavy, and her husband started snapping at the kids, who became more and more irritable as the time wore on. Roseanne considered the relative merits of abandoning her family and just walking the eighty miles back home.

By the time they stopped to eat, the tension level of the group was, to say the least, high. Roseanne, in an effort to alleviate the tension, began ambling slowly around the country inn where they had stopped to eat, and began talking leisurely to the children, pointing out the birds and flowers in an effort to get everyone to relax. Her husband, Steve, kept gritting his teeth and scowling, and was obviously having a terrible time. While eating, she slowed down even more; it helps her to relax. She chatted with the kids, buttered her rolls extra slowly, and sipped her coffee as leisurely as possible so they could all enjoy resting at dinner before getting back in the car. Steve by this time had reached a stage of near apoplexy and, feeling she could ignore him no longer, she said, "I know the trip is not what you wanted but shape up and quit making a fuss." He replied, looking quite genuinely surprised, that it was not the car trip that bothered him, though it had earlier, but the fact that she had been moving in slow motion ever since they got out of the car. In fact, he continued, she was "always" moving in slow motion, which he hated. It made him nervous and edgy.

I find it a telling story. Apparently Roseanne had been slowing down as a way of dealing with her own tension for years and had naturally assumed the same take-it-slowly method worked for Steve. So whenever she felt her family was getting tense or upset, Roseanne tried to slow down the works, partly for her own peace of mind and partly for theirs. Unfortunately, the very techniques which calmed her had been increasing her husband's tension. The more tense he got, the more she would slow down. She always thought she was married to a man who was very irritable (over nothing, it seemed), while he thought his otherwise normal wife had temporary spells of some relatively rare disease which prevented movement at normal speeds. It took them seven years to get the messages straight because she assumed she knew why he was nervous, so did not need to ask. He did not think it right to tell her she was driving him crazy when she so obviously liked to look at flowers, watch the birds fly, sip her coffee, or spend twice as long as he thought necessary on the daily paper. Neither felt the need to discuss the issue.

A client I was seeing several years ago almost left her husband because he frequently came home about a half hour late without telling her in advance or apologizing upon his return. The pattern had started about eight months before I met Mrs. Bennett and she was sure he was spending the extra time with one of the secretaries at his office. Her own father had left her mother for a secretary years before and she found the repetition of the event in her own life horrifying. I must admit, as she told the story, it sounded sad and ironic that Mrs. Bennett's worst fears were being met. After hearing her story, I inquired several times as to what Mr. Bennett gave as his reasons for being late and she repeated that he offered none. "He does not say." When I finally asked if she *asked* him why he was late every night she said no, that she didn't want to confront him;

she was afraid he would leave her if she pushed him. She was so sure he would have an excuse for his lateness there was no point in asking.[1]

Mrs. Bennett could not win. No matter what she did she could not be convinced of her husband's innocence. If she did not ask he could not prove his innocence. If she did ask she "knew" in advance he would lie. She would not believe him.

Mrs. Bennett feared her husband was involved with another woman because her father had been. Infidelity was a ready explanation with which she could explain his lateness. And that's what she did. A woman with different fears, different "readiness," might have worried he was in an accident the first time he came home late and would have, after he got home, asked why he'd been late. Suspecting hanky-panky, Mrs. Bennett was afraid to ask. We all have different concepts for coding late-from-work behavior and make different assumptions if our husbands or wives are a half hour late. We also differ in what we would think was happening on subsequent evenings if the pattern continued.

Of course interpretations of subsequent events depend heavily on the explanation received after the first delay. Mr. Bennett, it turns out, stayed late to avoid rush-hour traffic and get a little extra work done. He swears he told his wife when he decided to make the change, though she could not remember such a conversation. He wondered why she was often in a bad mood when he got home and could not understand why dinner was always ready the second he got in the door. He suspected she was angry but, not knowing why, was afraid to ask.

Not all people make negative interpretations in the absence of information. Some have strong tendencies to perceive things positively. Mrs. Brodsky is such a person.

Mr. Brodsky was attending night school and had been taking classes at night for several years before the Brodskys came to my attention. He had failed a course for technical reasons one semester because he forgot to withdraw after he stopped attending classes. There was no question he was not attending; the instructor had not seen him since the initial session. Mrs. Brodsky was home the morning the mail arrived and, not understanding the reason for her husband's failure, immediately called the university and was told her husband had not attended that course. When Mrs. Brodsky assured the secretary that her husband had attended the course—he left the house at 6:30 P.M. every Wednesday to do so, and did not return until after 11:00 and sometimes midnight—the secretary suspected she should not have been discussing the matter. It was too late.

Further scrutiny of Mr. Brodsky's record and of Mr. Brodsky (undertaken by his wife this time, not the university) showed he had been having an affair for the last three years with a woman he met at night school. During that time he had been signing up for two courses per semester and dropping one of the courses, thereby providing himself with a free night, and his wife with proof of his whereabouts in the form of two tuition receipts.

Mrs. Brodsky, a very understanding woman, had been happy to put up with her husband's absences in an effort to help him get through school. When he started coming home later and later in the evening (classes ended at 10:00), she never questioned the delay. It was obvious to her that going to school after working all day is a taxing and tiring endeavor. She assumed he either worked in the library for an hour before coming home or went out with friends for a quick drink after class. She was a trusting woman.

Like Mrs. Bennett in the previous example, Mrs. Brodsky had to find an explanation for her husband's delay. Both thought they understood what was happening. Both were wrong. But each woman would have looked quite different married to the other's husband: the trusting Mrs. Brodsky matched with a faithful, hardworking husband, and shrewd Mrs. Bennett insightful enough to be suspicious of her husband's deceitful behavior.

OBVIOUS CONCLUSIONS

All people at all times make meaning. This is true of children as well as adults. While we can only guess how most people construe events, children sometimes oblige by revealing more clearly than adults exactly how creatively they interpret the world around them.

Robby was three years old the day he was lucky enough to be taken out, along with six adults, to a busy and exciting delicatessen for lunch. He did beautifully while waiting for the waitress and sat very grown-up-looking, listening to all our conversation. Eventually the soup was served. Piping hot, it arrived plate by plate at the table and one by one we tasted the soup. Hardly aware of the fact we were repeating each other's remarks, first one and then the other of us said, "Hmm, it's hot. Please pass the salt." And slowly the salt made its way around the table. We would probably not have noticed the similarity of our responses had Robby not gazed up from his steaming bowl suddenly and asked in his high three-year-old voice for the salt. When we asked him why he wanted the salt, it seemed strange for a child that age to care about subtle seasoning, he informed us, in a tone filled with surprise and indignation because we did not

understand his reasons, that *his* soup was *also* too hot.
After all, it was so obvious.

THE FLOW OF INTERACTION

Interaction usually proceeds smoothly despite our errors. This occurs for two reasons. First, the responses of
those with whom we deal are generally ambiguous. As a
result, we do not notice that what they say or do is not
responsive to what we have done or said. For the same
reason, others fail to notice that our actions are not
responsive to their own.

Secondly, we adjust our responses to fit the actions
of others. When we see that others are off course we correct our responses to fit with theirs, or correct their errors
quickly so as to prevent further divergence. Ironically,
telling people that they have misunderstood a remark is
often considered impolite. (If we feel stupid when we
misinterpret, telling others that they have misinterpreted
suggests they have been stupid.) So rather than correct
misunderstandings, we sometimes shift the course of conversation to accommodate the error. The individual who
missed the point never knows he did so. The individual
who knows he did so is embarrassed by the knowledge
and soon forgets. The interaction looks correct. The flow
continues.

9

Making Things Happen

People do, of course, behave the way we predict a great deal of the time. One reason is that we influence the way they will respond by communicating (often nonverbally) what we expect. *Our own actions increase the chance of getting the behavior we expect.*

Imagine Ziggy, who tries, for the first time in ten years, to ride a bicycle. His wife shouts loudly out the door: "Be careful, watch out for cars, remember Morris (who spent four months in hospital after a bike accident)." Now it's obvious that his wife is genuinely concerned, well-intentioned, and afraid he will be hurt. Unfortunately, her remark increases the probability that exactly what she fears will happen. Though Ziggy starts out full of confidence, he is now worried not only about remembering how to ride, but about cars coming from all directions and the terrible consequences of an unlikely mishap. Being nervous and riding well are incompatible. The more fearful he is, the more likely he will fall. And each time he falls, he becomes more fearful. The irony of course is that what he fears becomes more likely the harder he tries to avoid it. And his wife's remark was hardly necessary in the first place. As a grown man, he knows enough to avoid cars while biking. Nonetheless, when he arrives home swearing never to ride again after narrowly avoiding an untimely and ignominious death under the wheels of an ice cream truck, she will have known all along it was going to happen. Didn't she warn him to be careful?

The same dynamic operates whenever we convey our fears or expectations to others: "Don't be nervous when you interview the boss" makes you so afraid of being nervous it's likely you will clam up with fright. "Don't be rude to my mother" makes you so self-conscious about how you are talking you are bound to sound both strange and unfriendly. "Don't let any of the big kids push you around" makes you so vigilant against being pushed around you're likely to preceive some highly ambiguous gesture as a threat and begin fighting. The list is endless.

We can also convey our expectations of success. Remarks such as "You usually do well on interviews" or "My mother is looking forward to being with you" convey an entirely different message from those above and increase the probability of very different behavior. After all, if your mother is looking forward to an evening with me she must think I am pleasant, entertaining, and clever. I'd hate to disappoint a woman with such astute judgment.

In each of the above instances, behavior is influenced by remarks concerning future events. The speaker need not be at the event in question. Because people see what they expect when circumstances are ambiguous, and social situations are always ambiguous, remarks about the future color their expectations, alter their perceptions, and influence future behavior. They, and we, are forever maneuvered by expectations.

Our tendency to elicit the behavior we expect from others, whether or not it is the behavior that we want, is especially evident with regard to children. Because their experience is limited, they develop theories about the world largely based on what *we* communicate to them. The self-fulfilling nature of our communications is relatively unameliorated by other learning. Children even more clearly than adults live up, or down, to our expectations.

SELF-FULFILLING EXPECTATIONS

The theories we form about children even before they are born illustrate the point. We anticipate they will be cute or homely, smart or dull, shy or outgoing, even before they are conceived. And while we acknowledge at these early stages that we are just guessing, the feeling that we are right is often strong. Many parents are "sure" about the sex of their child before it is born—and have been calling it "he" or "she" for several months before its actual appearance. Once the child can be felt moving in utero, the activity level of the baby, whether it moves a lot or a little, whether it moves gently or sharply, all contribute to parents' theories about its personality.

Given the wide range of activity possible and the fact that mothers differ in their sensitivity, there is great variety possible in the meaning given to in utero movement. Given a child who moves little, or is felt little by the mother (because she is physiologically insensitive, or is very busy and has little time to attend to her body feelings), several theories are possible: the baby might be considered (1) placid, (2) gentle, (3) weak, or even (4) sick if the mother believes a certain amount of movement, more than she feels, is normal.

The same process defines the child as healthy or sick if it is active. Even if it is not an unusually active child the mother may be particularly aware of its movements because she is particularly sensitive to touch or because she has little to do and spends a lot of time attending to the baby's movements. If the mother is unusually sensitive she may even find the kicking painful. In such cases the chance she will assume something is wrong with the baby (or herself) increases. So that a parent with an active baby might assume the child is strong, energetic, uncomfortable, eager to get out, or actually sick.

Activity level might also influence theory making about the sex of the child, as people often assume that boys are more active than girls—an assumption unsubstantiated by research. If parents assume their child is female, they might be more likely to interpret a high activity level as too high or, if they assume it is a boy, might interpret a low activity level as indicative of something wrong.

The way parents respond to their child is influenced by the assumptions they make before its birth as well as its actual behavior. All things being equal, a child who seems strong and active during pregnancy and births easily will likely be treated less gingerly than an infant who was hardly felt during pregnancy and had a difficult delivery.

Parents do not, of course, ignore clear differences. Some children are active, others aren't. But parents' theories about their children influence the way they interpret behavior, and affect the way they treat their children. Differences in treatment affect the children and increase the chances they will develop in accordance with their parents' predictions. The child who is seen as robust and treated vigorously will likely be exercised more than his counterpart who is seen as frail and/or ailing. Exercise alone might result in the physical robustness his parents imagined. In addition, a child who is treated heartily is likely to learn he is strong and able; a child who is treated gingerly is likely to conclude he is fragile. The children's theories about themselves will affect the way they treat themselves and what sorts of experience they seek out or avoid. As noted in chapter 2, a child who thinks he is healthy and strong is likely to seek out physical activities. He will eventually develop the strength and skills those activities encourage. It will appear with hindsight that his parents were correct in their evaluation. They knew he was going to be athletic.

CREATING PROBLEMS

In the previous example, parents' expectations operate to increase the chance of their child's being either frail or robust. Whether we consider frailty or robustness an asset or a problem is largely a matter of interpretation. We create our problems by the way we interpret and value events which occur.

An example is lack of sleep. For parents of infants, lack of sleep is often a problem. They frequently survive for several months on six or seven hours of regularly interrupted slumber. But the "problem" is often not the lack of sleep *per se*.

Children vary in the frequency with which they wake up during the night. They vary in that some wake only for feeding and others wake more often wanting to be soothed. They vary in the ease and quickness with which they return to sleep. Parents also vary. Some fall back to sleep easily after attending the infant; others remain awake for hours. Some need ten hours' sleep; others less than six. Some must get up at six for work;

others can sleep in until baby wakes and then take an afternoon nap. What one parent considers a problem, only
seven hours' sleep, another does not. What one considers
a solution, an afternoon nap, another does not. There is
obviously no one solution, as there is no one problem.

I can vividly recall spending hours with other new
mothers trying to solve the "sleep problem," but in writing this I have difficulty recalling why I was so concerned. I know, of course, I was concerned about being
tired. But I did not consider my fatigue a "problem to be
solved" during the first months of infancy. It was simply
a state I had to live in. After all, my child needed to be
fed often; I would live tired. But somewhere around the
fourth month, my definition of what was happening
changed. At about four months I learned that many children the same age as mine were not waking every three
to four hours. Some had slept through the night for the
last few weeks. It appeared quite suddenly I was not
dealing with something that had to be. Perhaps something could be done to alter my son's waking pattern.
Now I had a problem.

The perception that a problem exists, even before
one begins to define the problem, requires interpretation.
We must assume that the situation can be changed. After
that, our definition of what is actually happening will determine how we try to make those changes.

DISPELLING PROBLEMS

When it comes to child-rearing, toilet training is typically defined as a problem area. But the problem lies in
our perception of the task, a perception parents communicate to their children by the way they approach
their "training."

Recent writing regarding toilet training tells parents to wait until the child is two years old before starting training. That advice reflects doctors' and psychologists' theories about child development and about why training before two years is difficult: that the child may have poor muscular control before two years and that the child may have difficulty understanding what is required. Parents who assume their child is not maturationally or cognitively ready will defer training.

If we assume the child is ready to learn, but does not, it is common in our culture to see the parent-child relation as a battle of wits with each side fighting for control. Unfortunately, the "battle" interpretation, with its corollary assumptions about the child's stubbornness, spitefulness, or even resentment, is a trap. It does not lead to positive solutions. What do parents do if they think a child is fighting for control? To declare open warfare, with threats of punishment, is dangerous. If the interpretation is incorrect, the parents' own hostility is likely to generate hostility and anxiety where none existed. Even if the interpretation is correct, the display of hostility by parents is likely to increase the child's need to exert control, not lessen it.

An alternative solution is bribery. Rewarding a child for the correct behavior, giving candy for successful toilet experience, is a reasonable way of dealing with a child whom parents assume is manipulative. Unfortunately, parents who bribe often show they think their child has control and appear resentful. They generally treat the child as an enemy rather than a person with whom cooperation is possible. The risk of turning a perfectly cooperative child into an enemy should not be taken lightly.

But if the child is ready to be trained and understands what is expected, why isn't he trained? Victor, a neighbor's child, had been toilet training successfully in a short time but then reverted to wetting his pants. As he obviously knew how to do it right, Mrs. Marciello saw his refusal to cooperate as exactly that—a refusal to cooperate. She and Victor were having some terrific fights.

In desperation, Mrs. Marciello bought a book on toilet training which guaranteed results in one short day.[1] The authors of that book, both psychologists, have a theory about learning quite different from that described in chapter 2. They believe, along with many psychologists, that learning occurs when a child is rewarded for a particular behavior. When no reward occurs, no learning occurs. I generally find the theory ridiculously simple and not at all descriptive of learning that I have witnessed where frequently there is no reward. Nonetheless, Mrs. Marciello began to follow the recommended procedures and rewarded her child profusely every time he successfully used his potty: "I am so happy, I am so proud, Grandma and Grandpa will be so proud, Big Bird will be so proud," etc. At the end of the day Victor was retrained and it was clear that if his mother maintained a high level of praise ("reinforcement," in the jargon of psychology) he would not again revert.

Having watched the miracle, I was just about to discard years of theorizing and analysis and convert to a reward theory of how children learn (the evidence for the strength of the theory seemed strong) when Victor supplied an alternative explanation. Looking up happily at the end of the day, he smiled broadly at his mother, gave her a big hug and said with wonderment and puzzlement, "It sure makes you happy when I go in the potty." Obviously he had his own theory about what was happening that day and why he was behaving as he was (to please mother) that was not at all related to her or my assumptions.

What psychologists call reinforcement and parents

call bribery is often the same behavior given a different label. The behavior of parents who say to a child, "I'll hug you if you go to the potty," is not very different in appearance from the behavior of the psychologist who praises, hugs, and plays with the child after he goes to the potty. The difference is primarily in the way parents and psychologists construe what they are doing and how they convey it to the child. What they say to the child influences what the child learns from their behavior.

Parents in bribing situations do not think they have real control over the child; they bribe because they cannot get control without bribing. And they convey to the child that they are out of control, which strengthens the child's sense of control and gives him the confidence to try for control in the future.

Psychologists who "reinforce" young children assume they are in complete control. All they have to do is provide the proper reinforcement and they can get whatever behavior they like. So they convey to the child that he is not the boss, they are. And the child seems to learn that life is better, that he can get what he wants, by doing what others like, by cooperating.

The situation is analogous to the now classic cartoon in which a psychologist is seen standing over a Skinner box. A Skinner box is designed so that animals who perform a required task immediately receive some food—reinforcement or bribe, depending on your view—for doing it. The psychologist looks very proud because he has trained the rats so well.

The caption, however, focuses on the rats' perception. They also look satisfied. One rat is looking at the other and says, with pride equal to the psychologist's, "Boy, have I got him trained. Every time I press this bar, he gives me something to eat."

10

First Things First

To interpret the world around us we test our theories about what might be happening. Because our own actions and the actions of others are affected by the hypotheses we test, the *order* in which we test them is important.

Consider the plight of Mr. Bell as he tries to account for the change in Mrs. Bell's behavior. The Bells have been married five years and have two children. Mr. Bell, a lawyer, recently received a promotion and became a partner in the law firm for which he works. He is now secure in his job and spends more time at home with his family, as he no longer needs to stay as late at the office or to work as much on weekends. Mrs. Bell, a speech therapist, worked full time until she had children and continued to work on a part-time basis until last year, when she returned to her full-time job. Mr. Bell describes the following recent change in his wife's behavior:

> *"I'm not sure what's happening. She used to like being home and cooking, and seemed happy to*

*have the family around. I would come home early,
around seven o'clock, one or two nights a week
and we'd have a good dinner, the kids would be
bathed, we would eat together and play with the
kids. It was very nice. I looked forward to those
nights. Now I come home and she doesn't seem
happy I'm there. I sometimes think of staying late
at the office just to avoid home. I hate thinking it.
My wife's in a bad mood when I get in. I think she
wishes I wasn't there. The kids are cranky and
want to eat. We hardly have a civil dinner. We
rush the kids to bed and even after they're asleep
we hardly talk. I want to tell Stella about my day
and she just wants to read or watch TV. We
hardly make love. I feel like I'm imposing when
we do. Stella isn't interested. And lately she's been
staying at work late for meetings. I wonder if she
has found someone else. I don't think she's having
an affair or anything like that. But I think she
might not be interested in me anymore. I can't
figure out what's happening."*

Several theories about Mrs. Bell's loss of interest
arise from Mr. Bell's speculation.

1. She is more tired than before because she is working
full time and the kids are at a more demanding stage or
because there are new and difficult problems at the office.

2. She used to have more time alone to read and watch
television when her husband worked several nights a
week. Now that he is home she has less "free" time for
such activities and watches TV and reads while he's
there. In addition, the demands he makes on her may
have increased; he has more time and is around more.

Her level of interest has not decreased; his has increased and she is busy.

3.   She is upset about something unrelated to Mr. Bell.

4.   She is upset about her relationship with Mr. Bell and is staying late at the office to avoid going home. This is the assumption we hear underlying Mr. Bell's description of the problem.

5.   She is losing interest in Mr. Bell and is having an affair with someone from her office.

It is also possible to combine several of these hypotheses, so that Mrs. Bell may be having an affair and is also tired because she has gone back to work full time. In such circumstances she probably would be tired. She might even have been having an affair for the last three years before going to work full time, but her husband never suspected.

Mr. Bell must set about testing these theories to see which fits. He always tests theories. Generally he does so quickly, nonconsciously, and unsystematically. He usually tests in whatever order they occur to him. But the order in which he tests is important; his actions while testing affect his interaction with others and influence the conclusions he draws.

Mr. Bell lists the possibilities. He decides to check the preferred alternatives first. He also considers the ease with which he can check the theories and concludes that in this case the preferable alternatives are also the easiest to check. He proceeds in the order listed.

Unfortunately, Mr. Bell is afraid to ask his wife why she is behaving differently. He is afraid he won't like the answer. He is already nervous that she does not care about him and won't risk asking. He is afraid he won't like the answer or believe her if she says she is just tired. He embarks on a nonverbal test of hypothesis one.

On Monday afternoon he calls his wife and suggests she not make dinner—he will stop at a local restaurant and bring home pizza. He also gives the children a bath and reads one a story before bed; not his usual habit. When his wife settles down with a book later that night he decides to make no fast assumptions about what is happening. He will give the test a few days to work. People who are overworked, he muses reluctantly, cannot be expected to recuperate after just an hour's help. The second night he is again more helpful than usual.

Obviously by the third night he will notice some change. Only a wife who is half dead could fail to respond to *his* change in behavior. If in fact she was tired she will appreciate his help and begin to show her appreciation. She may even go out of her way to create one of their old-style leisurely evenings as a gesture of her appreciation. At least she is likely to thank him for his help and perhaps ask why he is so suddenly, and delightfully, attentive. She is bound to show some appreciation, possibly enough to relieve him of the nagging anxiety that she no longer cares. She may even be shocked into noticing that *he* had undergone some change recently, and ask about his job, or his tennis game, or whatever she thinks might be relevant to his new generosity and attention. Mr. Bell may not need to test further.

It is possible, however, that Mrs. Bell, while happy that Mr. Bell now helps with the children, does not show enough appreciation to allay his anxiety. She may thank him profusely for his help, tell him what a difference it makes in her evening, settle down to read her book, and reject him sexually later that night.

After a few such evenings, Mr. Bell might investigate theory two. He will spend a few hours, examining his own behavior over the last few months to see whether *his* demands have suddenly changed. He may conclude that they have. In such a case the problem may completely disappear. The leisurely meals and intimate discussions may have been less important than the significance Mr. Bell attached to them. Reassured by his insight that the change in their relationship does not reflect a change in his wife's feelings toward him he may find he enjoys the new, if noisier, pattern.

But Mr. Bell may not remember what he was like a few months back; it's not an easy thing to remember. Refusing to shirk an investigation, he takes on a few extra cases which require him to work late for several weeks. He wants to see if changes in his behavior cause changes in his wife's behavior.

It is likely he will get a response that fits his theory. It is probable, no matter what her reason for inattention over the past few weeks, that her husband's return to long hours will jolt Mrs. Bell into talking to him when he is home. She has no other time to do so. Secondly, if he does not like to make love when tired, he will not ask and she will not reject him as often. Her response is likely to fit his theory.

If Mr. Bell is still not satisfied that he understands the change in her behavior he will test hypothesis three: that she is upset about something. Unlike theories one and two, theory three can only be tested by asking Mrs. Bell if she is upset, and why. He must consult his wife directly. Short of hiring a private detective, he must do the same for theories four and five.

He must accept her answer as truthful when he asks. It is certainly no help to him if, when Mrs. Bell confides she is distracted because her friend Mildred is sick, Mr. Bell decides she is lying. He must believe her if she says she is worried. He has time to doubt her explanation when Mildred recuperates and she remains distracted.

Assume that Mr. Bell does not find Mildred's illness an adequate explanation of his wife's distraction. He still feels rejected. He investigates theory four—that his wife is upset about their relationship. It is not clear how to test that assumption short of asking if it's true. If she says that it is and explains why she is unhappy, the situation may be redeemable. If she denies she is upset or insists she is worried about something else, an explanation that Mr. Bell rejected above, he is in a bind. He wants her to say she is not upset but sees a great deal of evidence which supports his assumption that she is: she doesn't pay attention, she is busy outside their home, and won't attend his office party. Her denial seems unsupported by evidence. He may not believe her.

His problem is a problem of trust.[1] If he trusted Mrs. Bell in the first place, trusted her devotion to him and love for him, he would not be theorizing about her loss of love and possible infidelity in the first place. If he was sure of her love he would not have generated theory four. We only test the theories we think probable. (Unless preoccupied by death, for example, he would not think she was terminally ill because she no longer cooks elegant dinners. It seems absurd.) Because Mr. Bell thinks it possible, and even likely, that his wife has lost interest in him, her denial will not be convincing. It may temporarily alleviate his anxiety, but simply saying that she cares will not convince him that she does. He may test theory five.

Theory five differs somewhat from the earlier theories. The first four are framed so that confirmation, occasions when the observed data fit the theory, either solves Mr. Bell's problem or suggests solutions. Mr. Bell can help Mrs. Bell get more rest. He can organize his schedule, or redefine his needs. He can be extra nurturant until Mildred gets better. The Bells can go to a marriage counselor if she is unhappy with him.

In contrast, the confirmation of theory five is of little help to him. He does not want to find his wife is having an affair. He wants to find she is not having an affair. He wants to *disprove* the theory.

Unfortunately, we can never disprove theories of this type. Just as we cannot disprove the existence of Martians on Broadway cleverly disguised as humans, or disprove the existence of invisible friends whom only our child can see, we cannot disprove the existence of Mrs. Bell's lover. We cannot prove he does not exist. Even a private investigator cannot prove she does not have a lover. The best he can do is say with reasonable certainty that she hasn't seen him lately.

On some level, accepting that Mrs. Bell does not have a lover requires an act of faith on Mr. Bell's part. And an act of faith will not help him remedy his problem: no dinner, no conversation, no attention from his wife. Theory five is less productive than the others because it offers no solution. It may lead to a crisis if he concludes she has a lover, and depends upon a sense of self-confidence Mr. Bell is lacking to conclude she does not.

Testing theories in the order of desirability has advantages. By starting with the preferable theory Mr. Bell increases the chance of seeing what he wants to see.

In addition, the assumptions he makes and his own actions while testing the preferred theories are positive. If he assumes she is tired, he helps out. If he assumes she is depressed or needy, he is nurturant. If he assumes she is preoccupied by problems, he is supportive. Even if his assumptions are erroneous, his behavior will have positive effects.

In contrast, his negative assumptions increase the

chance of negative interactions. When he assumes that others are angry, he acts belligerently. When he assumes they are unloving, he acts rejectingly. His negative responses to his negative assumptions begin a spiral downward. His actions influence the course of events and his conclusions.

Mrs. Meyers' efforts to get Mike to clean his room, an apparently unambiguous problem, also illustrate how the order in which people test theories affect the conclusions they draw. Mike is six years old, a generally friendly and energetic child, who like other children of his age has a strong propensity for dropping clothes on the floor instead of into the hamper, and leaving toys conveniently in whatever place he happens to lay them. Mrs. Meyers, who resents cleaning up the mess, finds it irritating and somewhat hazardous to leave Mike's room in the conditions she finds it. Recently she has become particularly upset. She "has told him a thousand times to get the clutter off the floor and he doesn't act as if he heard." He "ignores" her request. He counts on her cleaning up. She feels "used."

Why might Mike leave the clutter on the floor?

1. Mike may not see the clutter. To him the clothes, trucks, and construction pieces are a sort of free-form sculpture—something to play with and fondle the next time he has a few minutes to spare. If he saw "clutter," of course he would pick up the room. Didn't he move Mother's newspaper out of his way when she left it on the bed?

2. Mike knows what his mother means by clutter and has decided to leave things as he likes them. He sees no reason for picking up his toys. He doesn't know why Mother gets upset.

3.   Mike is angry at his mother (because she refused to let him sleep at Luis' house, or go to the movie, or eat pizza) and is getting back by refusing to clean his room.

4.   Mike expects someone else to clean up for him—he thinks it's his right. He is lazy and manipulative. This is the assumption we hear underlying Mrs. Meyers' complaint.

Mrs. Meyers' problem only seems unambiguous—she wants Mike to tidy his room. But she does not know why it is messy. Her implicit assumption—that he is using her —is in fact only one of several possible explanations for his behavior. The alternative hypotheses seem preferable. They are certainly preferable when one considers the effect that Mrs. Meyers' assumptions will have on Mike.

Assume for the moment that Mrs. Meyers tries to generate theories to account for Mike's behavior. Her implicit assumption, the one she has been making as she gets angrier and angrier, is number four: he is manipulative. She will think of that first and will eventually generate the other three. They may not seem "real" to her; surely a boy of six can see that his room is a mess and knows why she wants it clean. She will give them a try, but in her own order.

If she assumes Mike is manipulative she is likely to confront her son in anger. She has been telling him for months to tidy his room. What kind of child is he? Doesn't he understand the meaning of cooperation? She does so much for him and he can't even tidy his room. His sister, a much nicer child (why can't Mike be like her), tidies her room every morning. Her message to him is of anger, resentment, and dissatisfaction.

If Mike perceives himself as lazy and manipulative, his mother's behavior will seem appropriate—though it's difficult to imagine a child who perceives himself as lazy and manipulative. People usually imagine themselves with considerable virtue and have wonderful explanations for their failure to behave in a fashion which other people, usually parents or spouses, prefer. A child who *does* consider himself lazy and manipulative would not be moved to clean his room after such an outburst anyway. Lazy and manipulative people specialize in avoiding work and getting others to do it.

On the other hand, if Mike sees himself as innocent his mother's accusations will seem harsh, unjust, and rejecting. He may decide not to clean his room to show her he doesn't like the way she treats him. He is now angry.

Mrs. Meyers would be better off testing theories one or two first. If she assumes Mike does not see the mess, or does not understand why she wants it tidied, she will teach rather than fight with him. She will remind him to pick up each evening. She will point out his toys might break if he steps on them by accident—a perspective that would be meaningful to him. She will remind him, without anger, of what she wants him to do and thereby increase the probability he will internalize her values or at least clear a path to the bureau. She will convey that children have responsibilities and that he is capable of fulfilling them, thereby increasing the probability he will become responsible.

If Mike was trying to anger his mother by not cleaning his room (theory three), her constant reminders to clean the room, with no trace of anger or resentment, might convince him his strategy was not working. If his manipulations do not yield the desired payoff, Mike will be forced to express his anger directly, in words, and might even get a satisfactory answer from Mother about why she did whatever it was that angered him. Her assumptions affect his actions.

The dynamics are the same whether we are dealing with our husband's or wife's behavior, our infant's crying, or our boss's moodiness. In all cases there are desirable and undesirable theories which are more or less easily tested. Theories tested first will seem "correct" because they often fit the data.[2] We can increase the chance of seeing reality in ways we prefer by systematically examining our assumptions and testing preferable theories first. Equally important, by behaving in ways that fit with preferred theories, either while testing them or after testing them, we have positive effects upon the theory making and behavior of those with whom we interact.

11

Doing It in Groups

Readiness also affects our perception in groups. Our interpretations are influenced by our theories about the people present, and the events in question. The process is more complex but remains essentially the same as when two people interact.

Consider the Cole family. Mr. and Mrs. Cole have been married eighteen years, have three children, and often fight about money. Mrs. Cole thinks her husband, an accountant, is stingy. According to her, he does not let the family spend as much as they might, given his income. In turn Mr. Cole thinks Mrs. Cole spends too much money. According to him, she spends too much on almost everything and has no sense of value. The differences in their attitudes are a constant source of irritation in their otherwise satisfying relationship.

Mrs. Cole is home with her husband one evening and suggests that they go out to dinner; he makes a counteroffer—that they go to a film instead. Because they had a fight the night before (he again accused her of overspending, she accused him of being a tightwad) their differences about spending are ready to influence her interpretation of tonight's discussion. She thinks he wants to see a film because it is cheaper than going to a restaurant. Her response is affected by her perception. The choice between dinner and a movie seems symbolic; she fights harder than she might to get her way.

The interaction changes if we add Marty, their ten-year-old son, to the scene; we see how interaction in groups differs from one-to-one conversation. Mrs. Cole suggests to her husband that they go out to dinner. Marty interrupts and makes a counter suggestion—that the three of them see a film instead. He argues that his parents have promised to take him to a film, that this is a convenient evening and a good opportunity for the family to be together. Mr. Cole *then* says he would also like to see a film.

Mrs. Cole might respond quite differently to Marty's, in contrast to Mr. Cole's, suggestion that she see a film. Marty's presence and the way he has put the suggestion alters her frame of reference and the readiness of categories which affect her perception. She sees the family as a unit and herself as a nurturant parent. She will focus differently. She is less likely to remember her fight with Mr. Cole. Her views on seeing a film and her response will be entirely different.

Readiness can also be influenced by people who are not present. Imagine that Marty is not in the room when Mrs. Cole makes her suggestion. Mr. Cole reminds her they have promised to spend an evening with Marty (thereby creating a family-oriented view of the issue), and then suggests a movie. The presence of Marty in her mind might serve the same function as his presence in the previous example. Thinking about Marty might alter her perception.

SOCIAL PRESSURE

In the instance described above, the presence of
Marty altered Mrs. Cole's interpretation of events. In
other instances, his presence might work so that she *rein-*
terprets events—though his presence is not sufficient to
affect her initial interpretation.

Mrs. Cole remembers her fight with Mr. Cole and initially thinks he prefers the film to dinner only to save
money. But Marty's insistence that the family spend the
evening together combined with Mr. Cole's insistence
that he wants to spend the time with Marty, prompts her
to reconsider. She may decide her initial view was not
correct, she was judging Mr. Cole too harshly. It is
difficult to hold to her original theory in the face of a con-
tradictory consensus.

Mrs. Cole faces pressure of still another kind. Regardless of the pressure to *interpret* events in ways which are
congruent with others, she faces a real and much more
immediate pressure to *respond* in a desirable fashion. She
has been asked to see a movie. There is pressure that she
do so.

Mrs. Cole must respond to both Marty and her husband in ways that appear reasonable. That may be a
problem. She wants to take Marty to the movie and
wants to spend an evening with the family. But she
thinks Mr. Cole is backing Marty only because he (Mr.
Cole) wants to avoid eating out. She is in a bind. If she
refuses Mr. Cole, she cannot go to the movie with Marty.
If she goes with Marty, she has to give in to her husband.
To go with Marty while refusing to go with her husband
appears crazy.

The issue becomes more complex if we imagine the

Coles' daughter, Dinah, age twelve, entering the discussion. Dinah wants to see the film. But Dinah has a test tomorrow and Mrs. Cole thinks she probably should study more. Mrs. Cole now wants to take Marty to a movie, does not want to give in to her husband, and is not certain whether she should make Dinah study. The more people interacting, the more complex the interaction.

But complexity exists not only at the level of interpretation and decision making. Mrs. Cole must also communicate her decision to others. If she decides she will go to the movie the issue is simple. She simply says that she will go. If she decides she will not go she must communicate her decision to them. She wants Marty to understand that her refusal does not signify rejection. She wants Dinah to understand that she thinks it in Dinah's best interests to study. At the same time she wants to check whether Mr. Cole is really "using the children." But she does not want to discuss their fight in front of the children and does not want the children to think she is refusing the movie so she can go to dinner without them.

It is not easy to send three different messages at once. In one-to-one conversations, Mrs. Cole chooses the words she thinks her listener will understand most easily. She gears her choice of words so as to minimize misunderstanding and decrease the chance of offending her listener. With three people present, she must find the words that will be best understood by the group. The chance of someone misunderstanding is great.

Some psychologists think that groups (families are groups) operate as organic wholes, that group dynamics are different from individual psychology. They argue that the rules which govern group dynamics are different from the rules that govern individuals.[1] The assumption is incorrect. Groups consist of individuals who interpret the behavior of others according to the schemas they have available to them and the readiness of those schemas. Their responses are influenced by their interpretations and how they think what they say will be interpreted by the others. Group interaction is complicated by the fact that different people affect the readiness of our schemas in different ways. They alter the way we interpret events. We see things differently when we are with different people or with different groups of people. We also have different objectives when dealing with different people. Action is made more complex by our efforts to respond differently to people who are present at the same time and by our efforts to insure that they each understand us in the way we intend.

We *seem* to behave differently in groups and to be governed by group process. But the difference is apparent not real. The way we operate does *not* change, though our interpretations and our responses may vary. It is not the group *per se* that has that effect. Rather, our views of individuals in the group influence our theory making, our interpretations of events, our goals, and our responses in any given instance.

ACTIONS VERSUS OUTCOMES

Behavior in groups is complicated for another reason. It is difficult to predict the outcome of an individual's action when only two people are involved; the chance of correctly predicting outcome when three, four, or five people are trying to influence one another is even smaller. The chance of each person interpreting the other correctly and responding in desired ways diminishes as the number of persons in the group increases. Even when interpretations mesh, people acting together often create situations that no one would anticipate.

Imagine the Cole family at dinner. All of them are present: Mr. Cole, Mrs. Cole, Marty, Dinah, and the youngest child, Jason, age five. Jason asks the others at the table if someone will listen to him read. After dinner, father clears the table and goes to the living room. Dinah goes to do her homework. Marty loads the dishwasher and then leaves the room.

Jason, who has been doodling with Magic Markers while waiting to read, looks up suddenly. He does not remember seeing his mother for the last five minutes—she has been reading the newspaper in the living room while the others cleaned the kitchen. His father, brother, and sister were there a moment ago but now are gone. It looks as if they lied when they said they would help him read. He feels misled and deserted. But each of the others assumes someone else is working with Jason. No one abandons Jason; each simply assumes that someone else is with him. They are unlikely to notice he has been left alone because they cannot account for each other's location. If Jason does not confront them with the fact he has been deserted they will not notice. Since he thinks they do not care, he may not tell them.

The distinction between what individuals do, their actions, and the resultant outcome is significant.[2] It is relevant no matter how many or how few people interact. But the more people who are present, the greater the probability of divergence between the intent of the individual actors and the resultant group process.

Dinah and Marty, for example, might each approach their father for help with their homework. They happen to choose the same moment to ask for help and each needs help "immediately." Their actions may precipitate a conflict which neither intended and which could not have been predicted from their individual actions. Nonetheless, the conflict appears unavoidable when their actions are taken together. Similarly, the pleasant circumstance in which two family members decide simultaneously they would rather play chess than continue watching television occurs from the confluence of their separate decision processes and could not be anticipated from their independent thoughts or actions. Neither, of course, could the response of the third member, who is left alone by the television and would rather have some company.

THINGS GOING WRONG

If the above examples suggest that the unexpected outcomes of individual action lead more often to negative than to positive consequences, that is not a false impression. There are, in any instance, more ways for things to go wrong than for things to go right. I owe a thanks to Gregory Bateson for his elegant clarification of why this is so.[3]

As Bateson points out, there are many ways for things to go wrong simply because we define events in such a way that few alternatives seem right, while an infinite number of other possibilities seem wrong. As an example, Bateson uses his daughter's efforts to keep her room neat. Because there are only one or two "correct" places for any item, and an infinite number of incorrect places for each item, the likelihood of a piece of clothing or a toy being in the wrong place is significantly greater than the probability of that item being in the right place. It is a simple statistical fact. If we define what is acceptable narrowly, the probability of events fitting our definition of acceptability is small. The more narrowly we define the acceptable category, the more likely events will go wrong, as opposed to right, as regards the dimension in question.

The application of this observation to interaction is intriguing. The more broadly we define behavior as acceptable, the more likely we are to find things going acceptably. The lesson is clear.

If we want our children to clear the table after dinner we are more likely to see them as fulfilling that obligation if we define clearing a bit less meticulously than we would for adults, and define after dinner so that they have a few minutes' leeway should they receive a phone call and get engrossed in conversation. If we insist they do a perfect job, and do it immediately, the probability that they will not increases.

Ironically, the fact that things go wrong more often than right applies most potently to group interactions. It is difficult enough for two individuals to understand each other clearly. Getting two or three individuals to interpret correctly is even less likely.

Again the difficulty reflects nothing more than probability. Assume that the chances of understanding someone correctly are 50–50. If Mrs. Cole is talking to Mr. Cole, he has a 50–50 chance of correctly interpreting her remark. If Marty is also present, he also has a 50–50 chance. But from Mrs. Cole's perspective the chance that *both* of them will understand her is now reduced to one in four (.50 for Mr. Cole times .50 for Marty). If we add Dinah to the conversation the chance that *all three* will understand her correctly is reduced to one in eight (.50 × .50 × .50).

If they do understand her correctly, the chance that all three of them find what she says acceptable is not great. If the chances are 50–50 that each will find her answer acceptable, the same problem arises with regard to interpretation. If she is talking to Mr. Cole, she has a

50–50 chance he will think what she says is acceptable. If she is talking to Mr. Cole and Marty, her chance is one in four they will *both* find her remarks agreeable. The difficulty multiplies with the number of persons present.

IMPLICATIONS

We might survive group interaction with greater peace of mind by applying what we know of information processing to the way we act.

1. *Context and focus.* Our perceptions of people and events vary from day to day, place to place, and group to group. We are influenced by the things and the people around us. They influence us by affecting the accessibility of categories we use to interpret events we encounter. We cannot eliminate such influence. Nonetheless, by recognizing that it exists, we can take precautions.

We think different thoughts in different situations. In making decisions that have lasting significance we want to know what we think at this moment, at this place, and also what we are likely to think later. Buying an encyclopedia seems like a great idea when the salesman suggests we focus on our children's love and appreciation, the brilliance they will obtain through high school, and the high salaries they will earn as adults because we have made the purchase. After the salesman leaves, we focus our attention on other variables—that our children will not get new bikes because we bought an encyclopedia, that they are under six years old and too young to read it, that the interest we pay on the purchase doubles its price.

The example seems farfetched, but the process is commonplace. Salesmen, like our families, friends, and colleagues, influence our perception by focusing our attention on particular aspects of events and altering the readiness of either parental, connubial, fraternal, or economic viewpoints. As a result, we perceive events differently in the various contexts they work to create. Considering alternative contexts before we make decisions decreases the chance we will be overly influenced by factors which will later seem irrelevant.

2. *Adequacy.* Things go wrong because we define situations in ways that increase the chance that they will. Things do not go wrong solely because we, or others, are helpless, hopeless, stupid, or malicious (though we sometimes are). When several people are together, things will happen that were not intended. We must live with it.

We can, however, define acceptable behavior more broadly. The broader our definitions, the greater the probability of getting behavior we find acceptable. The effect of definitional change increases as the number of people interacting grows.

Consider Mrs. Cole's dilemma. If the chance is .50 that each person will find her response adequate, the chance is only one in eight (.125) that *all three* will do so. But if each person becomes slightly more accepting (from .50 to .60) Mrs. Cole's chance of pleasing all three increases to better than one in five (.60 $\times$ .60 $\times$ .60 = .216). A broadening of their range of acceptability to .70 increases her chance to almost one in three (.70 $\times$ .70 $\times$ .70 = .329). If they are more accepting, she has a better chance of pleasing them and they have a better chance of being pleased.

It is a very profound effect. By defining our goals and expectations in a somewhat looser fashion, we radically affect our perception of success and failure, and our tendency to perceive events as pleasant or unpleasant.

The effect of such change is particularly pronounced in group interaction, though it also works in one-to-one situations and when we, in isolation, consider whether our rooms are tidy or the letter we have just received is adequate.

On top of this, our definitions affect the frequency with which we encounter discrepancies from expectations, the way we account for discrepancies, and the actions we take based on our interpretations.

Recall Mrs. Meyers (chapter 10), who tests theories in an effort to determine why her son, Mike, is not cleaning his room. If she defines "clean" in a particularly fastidious way, her chance of seeing the room as clean decreases compared to her chance if she is more casual. At the two extremes (fastidious versus casual) the chances vary greatly as to whether the room would be an issue in the first place, whether she would see improvement after her first request to Mike, and whether she would see improvement over time as she tests alternative hypotheses.

Mrs. Meyers keeps looking for improvement as she runs down her list of theories in order of preference. Her failure to see improvement leads her to test subsequent, and less preferred, theories. The more rigidly she defines improvement, the less likely she is to see change when she wants it, the more likely she is to continue testing alternatives. Her reluctance to see improvement (because she is fussy) increases the probability that her later and nonpreferred theories will appear correct. If she lowers her standards, she sees improvement earlier; her preferred theory will seem correct. Lowering her standards actually affects how she *interprets* Mike's behavior. It not only affects whether she thinks the room is clean, but influences her understanding of why it isn't.

3. *Ripples.* Deciding that something is wrong is like dropping a pebble in water. It creates ripples in our own minds which often affect others. Slight changes in the way we define acceptability can significantly decrease or increase the spread of ripples.[4]

The effect of such ripples is especially great when several people interact. Because the responses of one person are interpreted by several others, the effect of individual behavior is magnified in group interaction. As we have seen, the magnification occurs at several levels. For this reason, ripples become tempests and tempests become storms with virtually no provocation and certainly little effort on the part of group members.

There are, of course, no easy solutions. We continue to test hypotheses, to interpret events around us. We can decrease but not eliminate the chance of errors. But altering our theories about why error occurs changes the way we handle error when it arises. The recognition that things often go wrong from the sheer weight of probability affects the way we interpret errors when they occur. Attributing even a portion of error to chance affects both our behavioral and emotional response to error when it occurs. Recognizing that anger is frequently inappropriate, there are times when no one is at fault, we are more likely to respond with grace and possibly even humor to the botches and blunders we encounter. Whereas anger generates a spiral of anger and hostility, humor generates a cycle of humor and perspective. Because the impact of our responses is magnified by the number of people present, changes in interpretation are significant.

AMBIGUITY
AND
REALITY

12

Fast Change

There are different theories in psychology about how people change and how hard it is to change. The differences between these theories is not trivial.

At lunch recently, Patsy, an anthropologist, mentioned she was doing transactional analysis and said she was very excited about how fast she was changing. Transactional analysis was teaching her about the scripts she had acquired early in life, and she was learning to reject those scripts and to choose, as an adult, the kind of life she wanted—to rescript herself. She mentioned her therapy because it seemed to her that learning new scripts was somewhat akin to changing cultures. She was learning new rules about what things mean, and about what responses were appropriate given the new meanings.

An interesting discussion followed. A Freudian in the group, who rejected the idea of scripts as too simplistic an explanation of human behavior, asked the anthropologist whether she didn't really believe that her behavior was "motivated" rather than scripted. The implication of the question, based on a Freudian conception of mind, is that everything we think and do, even when we don't like our own behavior, is deeply motivated by unconscious desires. It suggests that change is not nearly so easy as the anthropologist would think because unconsciously we want to continue in our old patterns. At issue in the discussion was which theory of psychology was right.

To my mind both the anthropologist and the psychologist had missed an important point. Psychologists and psychiatrists do not know for certain why people change when they do or how to create situations in which change must occur.[1] If they did, there would not be several different theories of therapy, just one basic formulation which always worked, that all therapists would learn.

It is futile, given our current knowledge, to argue whether people are really scripted or really motivated by unconscious desire. It is more important for therapists and patients to focus on the effectiveness (and pleasantness) of techniques used by different therapies. The truth of their underlying theories and the adequacy of their techniques are not the same.

The problem is analogous to many situations described earlier in this book. We respond to situations according to our theories about what is happening. If what we do "works," we assume our theory was correct. But the accuracy of our theory has little to do with the adequacy of our action. Our actions might work for reasons which have little if anything to do with our assumptions. The same is true for therapies.

Psychiatrists and psychologists develop theories about the mind and devise therapies based on their theoretical assumptions. When the therapy works they assume that their theories are correct. But the value of a treatment may be unrelated to the therapist's underlying assumptions.

In therapy, the issue is change. The attitudes therapists convey to patients about the *likelihood* of change may be more important than the underlying theory upon which their therapy is based. Assumptions about change might in themselves have very different effects upon clients.

For the last thirty years, the mental health profession has been dominated by Freudian theory—a complex and somewhat varied body of assumptions about the nature of mind and the unconscious. Several points concerning Freudian-based therapies are of interest.

Psychotherapists who work within the Freudian framework tend to call their clients "patients"—small but interesting point with significant implications. A person who sees himself as a patient, which suggests he is "sick," not working right, and in need of help and medication, treats himself very differently from a person who sees himself as a client. A client is a healthy, functioning individual, in need of someone's specialized services to solve a temporary, though perhaps long-term problem; much as we go to accountants during tax time. The moment someone sees himself as sick, he loses confidence in his judgment (if he is sick it isn't easy to know which parts are working right and which parts aren't) and relies heavily on his doctor. The doctor knows what is best for him. In contrast, a client knows what he wants, knows what is best for him, and consults an expert about the best way of attaining his goal. Because lack of confidence in one's own judgment is often a major symptom of "neurosis," simply labeling clients as patients may be a hindrance to change.

Secondly, Freudian theory assumes that behavior is motivated—by which they mean we want to do, perhaps unconsciously, even those things we do not experience ourselves wanting. A Freudian therapist would assume that Patsy, a woman who wants to marry but consistently fights with her lovers when they get serious, has an unconscious desire not to marry. Patsy and a Freudian therapist would spend many hours analyzing and looking for early determinants of her fear of marriage. She will learn that her fear is deeply rooted in the past, which implies it is hard to change—a basic Freudian assumption. But believing change is difficult and slow increases the chance it will be difficult and slow.

In contrast, transactional analysis might teach Patsy that she was "scripted" as a child not to marry. She may have been told she is not the sort of woman men find attractive, that it is her job to take care of her parents, or that men only marry so someone will do their laundry.

Transactional therapists do not make a big fuss about the unconscious. Patsy may not have been aware of her early scripting, but transactional therapists assume it is easy to help her discover her scripts, and also assume that once the script is known it is relatively easy to free her from early scripting. Of course nonconscious processes are important in both transactional analysis and Freudian-based therapies, but they make different assumptions about the nature of nonconscious processes and the ease with which they can be altered. These differences in assumptions are conveyed to clients and will affect their behavior.

In transactional analysis Patsy might learn that she fights with her lovers because she thinks they will leave her anyway (she is not the sort of woman men marry). She fights to reduce her anxiety about their impending departure. If she picks the fight, she maintains control. If they leave before she gets dependent, it is not so bad. She learns her old scripts are destructive—there is no reason for men to leave her—if she would only stop fighting.

Behavior therapists also assume it is easy to facilitate

change. To the behaviorists, what we do is controlled by the rewards and punishments we receive from the environment. We learn to hit a tennis ball correctly because we are rewarded when we do it right; we score a point. We learn to swim correctly because we are rewarded when we do it right; we stay above the water, or make it across the pool faster with less effort. We learn social skills in the same way. We are rewarded for speaking clearly, being polite and inoffensive, or having a good sense of humor. People want to be with us. People who have not learned social skills are, according to behavior therapists, people who were rewarded early in life for inappropriate behavior. They continue to behave inappropriately because they do not know any other way. Though it seems obvious to others there are better ways of doing things, ways of getting more rewards, the person in question fails to see alternatives and continues in old patterns, even when they don't pay off. Such people often escalate the old and ineffective patterns when they don't get rewarded, because they assume they are not trying hard enough.

A behavior therapist might argue that Patsy, who fights with her lovers, was rewarded as a child for fighting. Perhaps her parents paid little attention to her unless she was disruptive. By being disruptive she could get their attention, and also see if they cared about her. Her behavior with lovers might reflect that technique. In fact, she probably does get extra attention from her lovers when fighting with them, so that they actually reward her fighting up until the time they leave.

Without discussing unconscious processes, a behavior therapist would teach Patsy alternative behavior patterns. He might help her practice new behaviors, or reward her for positive responses so she will respond positively in the future. His assumption that change is simply a function of rewards, and is not motivated, makes therapy fast and simple. He conveys to clients that they will not be burdened very long with whatever behavior they wish to change.

What I do not like about behavior therapy is its assumption that behavior and behavior change are controlled by rewards given us by others. The behavior therapist assumes his patient becomes more nurturant because he has rewarded her nurturant behavior in his office. He thinks that it is the reward, not the fact that he suggested and practiced alternative actions, that resulted in the change. For the client, that difference is crucial. If she shares the therapist's viewpoint, next time she has a problem she will go to a therapist so he can reinforce her more functional responses. She believes she is dependent upon him or someone else for further change. She thinks she cannot do it alone. In fact, she can; and would feel better about herself if she knew that. She may have needed his assistance in generating alternatives. But once she thought of alternatives she could achieve the same goal with a little practice, a lot less expense, and a feeling of self-control that would affect her future.

All therapies work by suggesting alternative explanations to clients who are locked into old and often limited ways of interpreting experience. If therapy is successful, clients come to perceive themselves and their situations differently. By offering new interpretations, therapists increase their clients' range of alternatives and their chances of finding responses that work. In turn, the clients' new behavior affects the theory making and the responses of those with whom they interact, in ways which support their (the clients') new assumptions.

Do-it-yourself books work the same way. They offer readers alternative explanations and suggest alternative responses. Some of the alternatives work for some of the people some of the time.

Several do-it-yourself books suggest that parents and teachers reflect (paraphrase and repeat) their children's comments in an effort to convey to their children that they understand them, and to verify that they are interpreting their children correctly.[2] If your child says, "I hate you for making liver," you might answer, "Right now you are mad at me." The author suggests, quite rightly, that that is preferable to something like "Shut up and eat your liver," a remark guaranteed to generate a lot of fruitless anger. It is also good, he argues, to show you are aware of and accept your child's frustration and anger.

Unfortunately, what appears to be a fine alternative does not always work in practice. It's not what we do in our dealings with others so much as their interpretation of our behavior that counts. My own child asked why I was "repeating" everything he said as soon as I tried reflecting. Of course, I was not repeating everything he said, but I was "repeating" more than I used to, and he noticed the change.[3] He felt angry and frustrated. He had interpreted my behavior change (we cannot *not* interpret) and, being three years old, concluded I was mimicking. Unfortunately, the interpretation he made did not match the meaning the author and I thought he would make. There is always a risk in assuming we know the effect our behavior will have on others.

The danger in following any advice blindly is wonderfully illustrated by Paul, whose daughter got angry because, after he read about reflecting, he "did not answer" her. When she started crying, or throwing pillows at him for some long-forgotten affront, he would tell her she was angry. But she knew she was angry. It seemed clear to her, if not to him, that crying and throwing pillows means "I am angry." She wanted to know why he did what he did, and whether he would do it again. She wanted an answer. When she complained, crying louder, that he was not answering, he said, "Now you're angry at me for not answering." He'd read the book and figured that reflecting just took a little longer to work with some children than with others. The process continued in a downhill spiral for several days until he finally figured out that the expert advice simply wasn't working.

He might have done better with another book, popular at the same time, which suggested almost the opposite technique. According to its author,[4] if your child gets off the school bus cranky, you should interpret his cry with what was "really happening." You might try "You had a bad day at school today" or "You had a bad ride home, didn't you?" But what if he didn't have a bad day at school, or a bad ride home? What if he is hungry? Why should you suggest that school is a problem or that you know what's wrong when it's just as easy to ask? You may not believe him when he tells you he is crying because a Martian came down and grabbed his lunch box, but that may be as accurate an explanation as a totally uneducated guess.

I object to therapies, how-to-do-it books, and almost any other helping program that establishes either the author, the therapist, or guru as expert. Because we all interpret events around us, and interpret with a great deal of originality, creativity, and often idiosyncrasy, it is not easy to know what others are doing, or should do. I do not know how you will respond to the excellent advice I offer, or how your behavior will be interpreted by others.

There is danger in taking advice blindly. If we do not do our own thinking we tend to be passive when things do not go as we want. We often continue to follow advice that does not work, or return to experts for new advice that will. But "experts" are only experts at generating theories. Some "experts" simply generate the same theory over and over again, applying it to a variety of different problems. Sometimes their theory works and we feel as if we've found a good expert. When it doesn't, we switch experts to find a theory that does. It is true that some people are good at generating alternative frameworks; they help us see things in more productive or more satisfying lights. They should be cultivated. Unfortunately, our culture assumes only experts can do that. Like other assumptions, it increases the probability that what it purports to be true will come true. We do not try to generate alternatives, run to experts to run our lives and, meeting failure, assume our only alternative is to try harder to find a better expert. It's not a productive or satisfying assumption.

Therapies and self-help books often fail to acknowledge that people make meaning of events. Sometimes therapies fail because the meanings we take from them are different from the meaning therapists try to convey. At other times, therapies are successful because they suggest interpretations that were previously unavailable to us. Their alternative views are helpful. The more theories available to explain our own or other people's behavior, the greater the chance we might interpret and respond in ways which work.[5,6]

13

Truth and Consequences

A<small>s</small> meaning makers, we have responsibility for our lives. We are not passive. We select alternatives from the theories that we ourselves generate. Our interpretations affect what we feel and how we act.

CHOICE AND RESPONSIBILITY

Of course, we do not live in a vacuum. We are influenced by real events. But we do have freedom to interpret and responsibility for how we interpret, more leeway and more responsibility than we generally acknowledge.

Consider Mr. Bell (chapter 10) as he tries to figure out why his wife, who returned to work full time, has been acting differently. His conclusions are influenced by her behavior, by his own theories, and the order in which he tests them. Another man might interpret differently.

Mr. Bell's *perception options*	*Emotion options*	*Behavior options*
She is tired.	happiness; relief; sadness; irritation	read a book; make dinner; go out alone; badger her to go out; go out with a friend; etc.
She does not love him.	anger; depression; longing; anxiety	shout; leave; sulk; go to a therapist; beg; worry; have an affair, etc.

Mrs. Bell also makes choices. At the start, she chose to return to work. Then she interprets Mr. Bell's response to her decision, and responds to him.

At each stage, Mr. and Mrs. Bell are equally responsible for their interaction. Each interprets the other's behavior and *chooses* to act in a particular fashion. Because they have choice, they are responsible for the choices they make; that responsibility cannot be apportioned.

The Bells create their options by interpreting events. This is significantly different from the view that each sees what is actually happening, is "overcome" by *the* appropriate emotion, and chooses between one or two culturally appropriate responses. The first view suggests creativity and independence, the second passivity.

The Bells do not merely react. They act upon events they encounter. They make choices in almost every situation; even when options are limited. They interpret events though they often cannot control them, and take action within the (often limited) range available to them.

Even six-year-old Mike Meyers (chapter 10) has, despite the limitations of his age, the option of cleaning or not cleaning his room when his mother asks. He interprets her request, responds to his construction, and in turn makes meaning of her response to his action. He maintains half of their dialogue (even if he chooses silence) and, along with his mother, has responsibility for it.

Our culture has, for the last several decades, seen people as passive. It barely acknowledges choice or responsibility. The passive view comes from behavior theory which, as was noted earlier, attributes behavior not to choices people make, but to rewards they encounter. Under such a framework, the social structure takes responsibility for individuals and parents take responsibility for their children.[1]

The Constructive view presented here suggests that individuals have both choice and responsibility. It acknowledges that choice is always limited by circumstances. It is often severely (and sometimes improperly) limited by others—either by physical constraint or by lack of information.[2] Nonetheless, choice and responsibility exist even within narrow ranges.

We do not create "reality" in a vacuum. The environment is real, though it is ambiguous. Our interpretations are shaped by real events and it is foolish to ignore their influence. It is, however, also foolish to assume our actions are determined by our experiences. The environment exists. Happily, it influences but does not determine how we interpret or respond to others.

ATTACHMENT

The view that we make meaning has some startling implications. Our usual attachment to truth and fact is shaken. When it comes to meaning, truth may as well not exist. Neither Mr. nor Mrs. Bell can know the truth of their relationship. It is doubtful that there is one truth.

To begin, behavior is multidetermined. The Bells cannot know which of several factors primarily influence their decisions.

The second barrier to "truth" is interpretation. Regardless of the reasons behind Mrs. Bell's actions, Mr. Bell can see her actions only through his own theories. It's as if he were looking through a template; the only shapes he sees are those with which he starts.

Even when they fit events closely, his constructs cannot encompass whole events. His constructs focus on aspects of events, not events *per se*. When Mr. Bell says that Stella is his wife, that is correct. But she is far more than the wife he sees. She is more complex and probably different from what he imagines. There are aspects of her he has not seen because he sees her in particular and narrow circumstances, and because his own presence affects her actions. Large segments of her past are unknown to him. She is influenced by, and influences, people he has never met and may not even know about. Anything he says or thinks about her is a partial truth.

His view of his wife is, at best, incomplete. And might be wrong. But he is attached to facts. He thinks he makes decisions based upon them. Without facts how can he take action? If he doesn't know what's really happening, what should he do? What should he say to Stella about her job and about their marriage? Should he accept his secretary's invitation for a quiet lunch? He is in a funny spot. In the past he made decisions that he thought were based on fact, and attributed responsibility for his decision to facts. In the past he'd have had lunch with his secretary because it would have seemed clear (despite a lack of evidence) that his wife was having an affair. Suddenly it's not so clear. Now he has to decide about the lunch himself. It's a new ball game.

The view that we cannot know reality, that everything is ambiguous is not new. Hindu and Buddhist philosophy make similar assumptions. They argue that the reality we see is *maya* (illusion). Within that framework, enlightenment comes with an ability to watch the flow of events without attachment to the events themselves or to our interpretation of them.

Enlightenment according to Buddhism brings peace of mind, emotional tranquility, and a sense of oneness with the world. Within the Constructive framework we can see how this might be so. An "enlightened" Mr. Bell would become less possessive, less attached to knowing the "truth" about his wife's new schedule, and less attached to outcomes he knows are beyond his control. He sees that several different things might be happening.

To begin, the emotional pain he feels is diminished. He encounters fewer misfits from his expectations because he has fewer expectations. Those he has he holds with less rigidity and less desperation than he used to; he has learned they are constructions and is not so shocked to find he's sometimes wrong. He does not always like what happens. But his sense that his world is falling apart when people don't meet his expectations has lessened. It's not the world that's falling apart, just his constructions; and they have become more tentative.

Because Mr. Bell recognizes that his perceptions and interactions are in large part creations, his sense of isolation is lessened. He no longer sees a world-out-there in contrast to his self. The world that he sees cannot be separated from himself. He and it are part and parcel of a complex and circular relationship. He interprets events, responds to his constructions, and influences events. The relation between himself and the "outside" is of one piece. The outside that he knows is inside.

Indian ideas of oneness and nonattachment make no scientific sense within the traditional view that perception discloses reality. They make perfect sense in terms of recent psychological research and theory. In fact, if Indian philosophy had not introduced these notions recent research would eventually force us to do so.[3]

What Indian philosophy and Constructive Psychology force us to acknowledge is responsibility. They recognize the illusory nature of events and the interactive nature of social behavior. We do not simply respond to the flow of events because events do not "flow." More accurately, the flow is not passive. Events are affected by us, whether we choose to watch others act, choose to participate in the action, or try to alter the events in question. We are an integral part of the events and cannot, in fact, help but influence their course. "Watching the flow" is itself a choice for which we have responsibility; it is one of several options.[4]

METAPHOR

Within Hindu philosophy reality is *maya*. The flow that we see is *lila*, the play or dance of God. The following description of Hindu thought, written by Huston Smith, presents the metaphor beautifully:

> *The world as it now appears to us is* maya. *This word is often translated "illusion," but this is misleading. For one thing, it suggests that the world need not be taken seriously. This the Hindu would deny, pointing out that as long as it appears real and demanding to us we must accept it as*

such. Moreover, it does have a kind of qualified reality; reality on a provisional level.

Were we to be asked if dreams are real, our answer would have to be qualified. They are real in the sense that we have them, but they are not real in the sense that the things they depict necessarily exist in their own right. Strictly speaking, a dream is a psychological construct, something created by the mind out of its particular state. When the Hindus say the world is maya, this too is what they mean. Given the human mind in its normal condition, the world appears as we see it. But we have no right to infer from this that reality is in itself the way it so appears. A child seeing a motion picture for the first time will assume that the objects he sees—lions, kings, canyons—are objectively before him; he does not suspect that they are being projected from a booth in the rear of the theater. It is the same with us; we assume the world we see to be in itself as we see it, whereas in actuality it is a correlate of the particular psychophysical condition our minds are currently in. To change the metaphor, our sense receptors pick up only those wave lengths to which they are tuned . . .

Maya comes from the same root as magic. In saying the world is maya, non-dual Hinduism implies that there is something tricky about it. The trick, we see, lies in the way its materiality and multiplicity pass themselves off for being independently real apart from the state of mind from which they are seen . . .

The best we can say is that the world is lila, God's play. Children playing hide-and-seek assume various roles that have no validity outside *the game. They place themselves in jeopardy and in a condition in which they must make their escape to freedom. Why do they do this when they could become "free" in a twinkling by merely stepping out of the game? The only answer is that the game is its own point; it is fun in itself, a spontaneous overflow of creative, imaginative energy. So too in some mysterious way must it be with the world. Like a child playing alone, God is the lonely cosmic dancer whose routine is all creatures and all worlds. From the tireless stream of his cosmic energy these flow without end as he executes his graceful, repetitious movements.*[5]

Psychological theories of mind are also metaphors.[6] The behaviorist metaphor suggests that mind is like a switchboard. Connections are made between things "out there" (stimuli) and the individual's responses when the stimulus-response link is followed by reward. We look like mechanized stimulus-response machines to behaviorists because they "see" us as switchboards.

An alternative metaphor comes from new research. Like artists we create pictures, stories, and poems that fit events. The way we elaborate events, the stories and pictures we build around them determine how we feel and how we respond to events in question. The pictures we create may be complex or simple, black and white or richly colored. The focus might be sharp or soft, the field of vision short or deep; the frame will vary. The gallery of pictures and narratives we carry with us is our reality.

This view stresses creativity. It allows for romanticism and irony, passion and poignancy, a value system that emphasizes means as well as ends, feeling as well as function. As artists we create pictures. We credit our originality and ingenuity.

As artist-scientists, we make meaning from ambiguity. The way we make meaning and relate the portions of our creation determine the sort of life we lead and how we lead it.

Seeing ourselves as artist-scientists, we become aware of choices and start to make them consciously. Knowing that we choose affects the choices we make and how we make them. In short, recognizing that we "choose" to see what we see affects how we deal with and how we feel about the reality we create. The events and relationships in which we participate are, in large measure, of our own making. The challenge is to see what we make of the ambiguity that comes our way.

The dance analogy with which this book began expresses the feeling. It differs from Hindu metaphor in that the dance, the reality, is our own creation. The view that we are dancing reflects the constancy of change and movement in relationships. Our constructions determine how the music sounds and how the dancers look. The variations we jointly create add excitement and romance to the dance. We can choose the steps, alter the tempo, and influence the direction of movement. We are the dancers, the musicians, and the choreographers. The fact that we are each responsible for the steps we take makes the dance worth dancing, gives joy to the patterns, and a sense of poetry to the dancers.

Notes

Introduction: About This Book

1. Kuhn, T. (1962). Like other "revolutionary" ideas, the ones discussed in this book have evolved gradually; antecedents of recent research appear in related work, most notably by phenomenologists and psycholinguists. Acceptance of these ideas will be revolutionary despite their long evolution on the margins of our culture.

2. "Under the most rigorous controlled conditions of pressure, temperature, volume, humidity, and other variables, the organism will do as it damn well pleases." Bloch, A. (1979), p. 35.

3. The similarity between assumptions of Eastern philosophy and those arising from particle physics have been documented elsewhere. A particularly readable account of that relationship can be found in Capra, F. (1975).

4. For a historical discussion of the politics of psychology see Chorover, S. L. (1979).

Chapter 1: I Wonder What He Meant by That

1. Berger, P. L., and Luckman, T. (1967).

Chapter 2: The Child Is Father to the Man

1. Piaget, J. (1952).
2. Bruner, J. S. (1973).

3. Bruner, J. S. (1957).

4. Foschi, M., and Foschi, R. A. (1979).

5. Fyans, L. J., and Maehr, M. L. (1979).

6. Rosenthal, R., and Jacobson, L. (1968).

7. Meyer, W. U. (1979), and Cooper, H. M., and Baron, R. M. (1979).

8. Laing, R. D. who suggests these alternatives, calls the struggle over definitions of what is happening "the politics of experience." For further discussion see Laing, R. D. (1967).

9. Bem, S., and Bem, D. (1970).

Chapter 3: Ready, Get Set, See

1. For a provocative critique of traditional approaches to perception see Oatley, K. (1979).

2. Bruner, J. S., and Goodman, C. C. (1947).

3. Bruner, J. S., Postman, L., and Rodrigues, J. (1951).

4. Bruner, J. S. (1957).

5. McGinnies, E. (1949).

6. Solomon, R. L., and Howes, D. H. (1951).

7. On the relation of context to accessibility see Neisser, U. (1976), Bateson, G. (1972), and Goffman, E. (1974).

8. Miller, G. A., Bruner, J. S., and Postman, L. (1954).

Chapter 4: Feel This

1. For a more detailed treatment of this material see Katz, J. M. (1980).

2. Hebb, D. O. (1955), and Hopkins, J. R., Zelazo, P. R., Jacobson, S. W., and Kagan, J. (1976).

3. Schachter, S., and Singer, J. E. (1962).

4. Younger, J. C., and Doob, A. N. (1978).

5. Schachter, S., and Singer, J. E. (1962) and Schachter, S., and Wheeler, L. (1962).

6. Dr. Roy Schafer (1976) carries this argument even further. He says that emotions are not "things" at all, but rather processes. We should, according to Schafer, say "He responded angrily" rather than "He felt anger." The change from treating emotion as a noun to treating emotion as an adverb emphasizes the flexibility and choice in emotional responses.

Chapter 5: Ah Love

1. Material in this chapter appeared originally in Katz, J. M. (1976).

2. Although the concept of love in the *theological* sense has been around for a while, the theological concept of love bears little relation to romantic love. Romantic love is antithetical to theological love. Romantic love requires that the lover love one person to the exclusion of loving others. If one acted the same toward all people, no matter how loving that behavior, he or she would not appear to love in the way the romantic definition demands. For a theological discussion of love see Tillich, P. (1954).

3. For reviews of what little research exists in the area see Rubin, Z. (1973), and Elkins, G. R., and Smith, D. (1979).

4. Reiss, I. L. (1960).

5. Kagan, J., and Moss, H. A. (1962).

6. Regarding the perception of manipulation see Karniol, R., and Ross, M. (1979).

Chapter 6: Everybody Does It

1. Gerbner, G., Gross, L., Eleey, M. F., Jackson-Beeck, M., Jeffries-Fox, S., and Signorielli, N. (1977).

2. The relatively recent trend toward "growth" movements in psychology and the popularity of Gail Sheehy's *Passages* (1974), a book which emphasizes change over the life cycle, have introduced an idea of change which is new to our culture and not yet generally accepted. In fact, the sudden increase in our life expectancies may have more to do with today's life "stages" than social factors. When men expected to die at fifty they did not wonder at thirty-eight what they would do for the next thirty-five years. By the same token, middle-aged couples who now consider divorce, in earlier centuries knew that nature would likely intervene to save them that painful option. When life was shorter there were fewer years of change and few years of living with the consequences of those changes.

3. I am thinking here of research stemming from Rotter, J. B. (1966), and Seligman, M. E. P. (1975).

4. Consider the following articles in *one* recent issue of *Journal of Marriage and the Family* (1980, vol. 42): "The Gainful Employment of Women with Small Children"; "On the Effects of Wives' Employment on Marital Adjustment and Companionship"; "Necessity, Compatibility, and Status Attainment as Factors in the Labor Force Participation of Married Women"; "Postponing Marriage: the Influence of Young Women's Work Expectations." Try substituting the word "men" for "women" in the above titles.

5. Culture through language also defines the range, depth, and specificity of emotional experience for individuals in that culture. The Tahitians, for example, have no

word for depression and fail to differentiate between negative emotions generally. In contrast to our own culture, which has many words that distinguish between negative emotion, they do distinguish various kinds of positive feeling. (Levy, R. I. [1973].)

6. Hochschild, A. R. (1975).

Chapter 8: Doing It Together

1. In this context Mr. Bennett lacks credibility. See Sternthal, B., Phillips, L. W., and Dholakia, R. (1978).

Chapter 9: Making Things Happen

1. Azrin, N. H., and Foxx, R. M. (1976).

Chapter 10: First Things First

1. On the development of trust see Lindskold, S. (1978).

2. Paranoids are people who, when things go wrong, assume that someone is out to get them. It's a theory that often seems to fit the data, is difficult to disprove, and can easily, over the years, become very "ready." Complex mediating mechanisms like projection are not necessary to explain most "errors" of perception. What psychologists call projection is theory testing that is, as always, affected by introspection.

Chapter 11: Doing It in Groups

1. Regarding emergent group characteristics and the transmission of knowledge see "The Hundredth Monkey Phenomenon" in Watson, L. (1979).

2. On the distinction between praxis and process (events done by doers and those that have no agents) see Laing, R. D., and Esterson, A. (1964).

3.   Bateson, G. (1972).

4.   For an interesting development of the thought-as-ripple metaphor, see Patanjali (1955).

Chapter 12: Fast Change

1.   The problem arises for therapists because their clients' interpretations of events, not events themselves, lead to change. Therapists use a variety of techniques which increase the *probability* of change but cannot predict exactly when these techniques will be effective or know precisely why they are when they are.

2.   Gordon, T. (1975) and (1977).

3.   Gordon (1977) actually warns his readers not to "repeat." They should reflect the *meaning* of remarks made. But children who think they have expressed their anger clearly having said, "I hate you for making liver," find statements like "You are angry" repetitious.

4.   Ginott, H. (1973).

5.   One theory of change, congruent with the Constructive view, suggests that change occurs when the frame of perception alters: when the thing being observed is seen in a different light. Reframing perception, making some views more accessible than others, results in the creation of a new reality. (Watzlawick, P., Weakland, J. H., and Fisch, R. [1974], and Bandler, R., and Grinder, J. [1979].)

6.   For an earlier discussion of therapy and the construction of reality see G. A. Kelly, *The Psychology of Personal Constructs*. Kelly's therapy is based explicitly on the assumption that reality is interpreted. Recognizing that people construe events, Kelly (1955) saw psychotherapy as the restructuring of nonfunctional constructs.

Chapter 13: Truth and Consequences

1. In contrast, Jane Loevinger (1959) uses cognitive theory to account for the unavoidable failure of parents to establish tight control over their children. Children make meaning of their parents' actions; they do not always learn what their parents want them to. Consider parents who want to teach their children not to hit. Children who are hit (for hitting other children) might learn it is okay to hit. Children whose parents reason with them might learn that the offense is not very serious—they weren't even hit. Arlene Skolnick (1978) extends that discussion. She argues that parental control has been greatly overestimated in our culture and that responsibility for their choices might better be returned to children.

2. For a fuller discussion of social control see Neisser, U. (1976), p. 176–194.

3. This is not to say that Indian views of perception are exactly those proposed by recent research. While early Buddhists argued that the world is *maya*, they assumed that the perception of *maya* could be objective, that we could objectively agree on what the illusion looks like (Oliver, C., 1978).

4. The distinction between praxis and process (see chapter 11, note 2) clarifies the point. The flow can be seen as process. But process comes from praxis.

5. Smith, H. (1958), p. 82–84.

6. For a discussion of consciousness as metaphor (itself a metaphor), see Jaynes, J. (1976).

References

Azrin, N. H., and Foxx, R. M. *Toilet Training in Less Than a Day*. New York: Simon and Schuster, 1976.

Bandler, R., and Grinder, J. *Frogs into Princes: Neurolinguistic Programming*. Moab, Utah: Real People Press, 1979.

Bateson, G. *Steps to an Ecology of Mind*. New York: Ballantine Books, 1972.

Bem, S., and Bem, D. "Case Study of Nonconscious Ideology: Training the Woman to Know Her Place." In D. J. Bem, *Beliefs, Attitudes, and Human Affairs*. Belmont, Calif.: Brooks/Cole Publishing Co., 1970.

Berger, P. L., and Luckman, T. *The Social Construction of Reality*. Garden City, N. Y.: Anchor Books, 1967.

Berlyne, D. E. "The Influence of Complexity and Novelty in Visual Figures on Orienting Responses." *Journal of Experimental Psychology*, 1958, 55: 289–296.

Bloch, A. *Murphy's Law*. Los Angeles: Price, Stern & Sloan, 1979.

Bruner, J. S. "On Going Beyond the Information Given." In J. Anglin (ed.), *Beyond the Information Given*. New York: W. W. Norton & Co., 1973.

Bruner, J. S. "On Perceptual Readiness." *Psychological Review*, 1957, 64: 123–152.

Bruner, J. S., and Goodman, C. C. "Value and Need as Organizing Factors in Perception." *Journal of Abnormal and Social Psychology*, 1947, 42: 33–44.

Bruner, J. S., Postman, L., and Rodrigues, J. "Expectation and the Perception of Color." *American Journal of Psychology*, 1951, 64: 216–227.

Capra, F. *The Tao of Physics*. Berkeley, Calif.: Shambala Press, 1975.

Chorover, S. L. *From Genesis to Genocide*. Cambridge, Mass.: MIT Press, 1979.

Cooper, H. M., and Baron, R. M. "Academic Expectations, Attributed Responsibility, and Teachers' Reinforcement Behavior: A Suggested Integration of Conflicting Literatures." *Journal of Educational Psychology*, 1979, 71: 274–277.

Elkins, G. R., and Smith, D. "Meaning and Measurement of Love: A Review of Humanistic and Behavioral Approaches." *Humanist Educator*, 1979, 18: 7–12.

Foschi, M., and Foschi, R. A. "A Bayesian Model for Performance Expectations: Extension and Simulation." *Social Psychological Quarterly*, 1979, 42: 232–241.

Fyans, L. J., and Maehr, M. L. "Attributional Style, Task Selection, and Achievement." *Journal of Educational Psychology*, 1979, 71: 449–507.

Gerbner, G., Gross, L., Eleey, M. F., Jackson-Beeck, M., Jeffries-Fox, S., and Signorielli, N. "Violence Profile No. 8: Trends in Network Television Drama and Viewer Conceptions of Social Reality 1967–1976." Report (1977) available from the Annenberg School of Communications, University of Pennsylvania, Philadelphia.

Ginott, H. *Between Parent and Child*. New York: Avon Books, 1973.

Goffman, E. *Frame Analysis*. New York: Harper Colophon Books, 1974.

Gordon, T. *Parent Effectiveness Training*. New York: New American Library, 1975.

Gordon, T. *Teacher Effectiveness Training*. New York: Longman, 1977.

Hebb, D. O. "Drive and the C.N.S. (Conceptual Nervous System)." *Psychological Review*, 1955, 62: 243–353.

Hochschild, A. R. "The Sociology of Feeling and Emotion: Selected Possibilities." In Marcia Millman and Rosabeth Kanter (eds.), *Another Voice*, Garden City, N.Y.: Anchor Books, 1975.

Hopkins, J. R., Zelazo, P. R., Jacobson, S. W., and Kagan, J. "Infant Reactivity to Stimulus Schema Discrepancy." *Genetic Psychology Monographs*, 1976, 93: 27–62.

Jaynes, J. *The Origin of Consciousness in the Breakdown of the Bicameral Mind*. Boston: Houghton Mifflin Co., 1976.

Kagan, J., and Moss, H. A. *Birth to Maturity: The Fels Study of Psychological Development*. New York: John Wiley & Sons, 1962.

Karniol, R., and Ross, M. "Children's Use of a Causal Attribution Scheme and the Inference of Manipulative Intentions." *Child Development*, 1979, 50: 463–468.

Katz, J. M. "A Psychosocial Theory of Emotion." *Sociological Inquiry*, 1980, 50: 147–156.

Katz, J. M. "How Do You Love Me? Let Me Count the Ways. (The Phenomenology of Being Loved)." *Sociological Inquiry*, 1976, 46: 17–22.

Kelly, G. A. *The Psychology of Personal Constructs*. New York: W. W. Norton & Co., 1955.

Kuhn, T. *The Structure of Scientific Revolutions*. Chicago: University of Chicago Press, 1962.

Laing, R. D. *The Politics of Experience.* New York: Pantheon Books, 1967.

Laing, R. D., and Esterson, A. *Sanity, Madness and the Family.* New York: Basic Books, 1964.

Levy, R. I. *Tahitians.* Chicago: University of Chicago Press, 1973.

Lindskold, S. "Trust Development, the Grit Proposal, and the Effects of Conciliatory Acts on Conflict Cooperation." *Psychological Bulletin,* 1978, 85: 772–793.

Loevinger, J. "Patterns of Child Rearing as Theories of Learning." *Journal of Abnormal and Social Psychology,* 1959, 55: 148–150.

McGinnies, E. "Emotionality and Perceptual Defence." *Psychological Review,* 1949, 56: 244–251.

Meyer, W. U. "Academic Expectations, Attributed Responsibility, and Teachers' Reinforcement Behavior: A Comment on Cooper and Baron, with Some Additional Data." *Journal of Educational Psychology,* 1979, 71: 269–273.

Miller, G. A., Bruner, J. S., and Postman, L. "Familiarity of Letter Sequences and Tachistoscopic Identification." *Journal of General Psychology,* 1954, 50: 129–139.

Neisser, U. *Cognition and Reality.* San Francisco: W. H. Freeman & Co., 1976.

Oatley, K. *Perceptions and Representations: The Theoretical Bases of Brain Research and Psychology.* New York: Free Press, 1979.

Oliver, C. "Perception in Early Nyaya." *Journal of Indian Philosophy,* 1978, 6: 243–266.

Patanjali. *How to Know God: The Yoga Aphorisms.* Translated with a commentary by Swami Prabhavananda and Christopher Isherwood. New York: Harper & Bros., 1955.

Piaget, J. *The Origins of Intelligence in Children.* 2nd ed. New York: International Universities Press, 1953.

Reiss, I. L. "Toward a Sociology of the Heterosexual Love Relationship." *Marriage and Family Living,* 1960, 22: 139–145.

Rosenthal, R., and Jacobson, L. *Pygmalion in the Classroom.* New York: Holt, Rinehart & Winston, 1968.

Rotter, J. B. "Generalized Expectancies of Internal Versus External Control of Reinforcement." *Psychological Monographs,* 1966, 80.

Rubin, Z. *Liking and Loving.* New York: Holt, Rinehart & Winston, 1973.

Schachter, S., and Singer, J. E. "Cognitive, Social, and Psychological Determinants of Emotional States." *Psychological Review,* 1962, 69: 379–399.

Schachter, S., and Wheeler, L. "Epinephrine, Chlorpromazine, and Amusement." *Journal of Abnormal and Social Psychology,* 1962, 65: 121–128.

Schafer, R. *A New Language for Psychoanalysis.* New Haven, Conn.: Yale University Press, 1976.

Seligman, M. E. P. *Helplessness: On Depression, Development, and Death.* San Francisco: W. H. Freeman & Co., 1975.

Sheehy, G. *Passages.* New York: E. P. Dutton, 1974.

Skolnick, A. "The Myth of the Vulnerable Child." *Psychology Today,* 1978, 11: 56–58.

Smith, H. *The Religions of Man.* New York: Harper & Bros., 1958.

Solomon, R. L., and Howes, D. H. "Word Frequency, Personal Values, and Visual Duration Thresholds." *Psychological Review,* 1951, 58: 256–270.

Solomon, R. L., and Postman, L. "Frequency of Usage as a Determinant of Recognition Thresholds for Words." *Journal of Experimental Psychology,* 1952, 43: 195–201.

Sternthal, B., Phillips, L. W., and Dholakia, R. "The Persuasive Effect of Source Credibility: A Situational Analysis." *Public Opinion Quarterly*, 1978, 42: 285–314.

Tillich, P. *Love, Power, and Justice*. London: Oxford University Press, 1954.

Watson, L. *Lifetide*. London: Hodder and Stoughton, 1979.

Watzlawick, P., Weakland, J. H., and Fisch, R. *Change*. New York: W. W. Norton & Co., 1974.

Younger, J. C., and Doob, A. N. "Attribution and Aggression: The Misattribution of Anger." *Journal of Research in Personality*, 1978, 12: 164–171.

Index

AP